GRADE 3 GEOMETRY

Fun-filled Activities

An imprint of Om Books International

Point And Line Segment

Point – A point is represented by a dot [.]. It shows a definite position. We use letters of the English alphabet to name points.

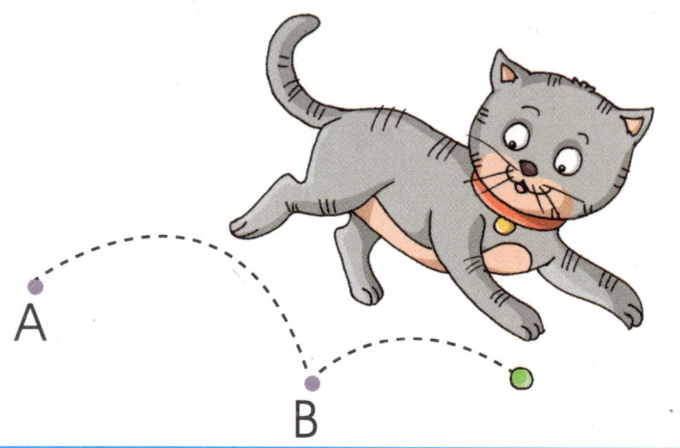

Line Segment – A line segment is a part of a line. It has two end points. The line does not go further than the length between the two given points.

$\overline{AB}$ is a line segment and the symbol to show it is written like this: $\overline{AB}$.

QUICK CHECK
Whenever two line segments meet, they meet at a point.

Look at the picture and tick (✓) the correct option for the questions.

1. How many line segments are there in the picture?

☐ 20 ☐ 17 ☐ 13

2. How many line segments does the middle triangle have?

☐ 5 ☐ 4 ☐ 3

3. How will you represent line segment BC?

☐ BC ☐ $\overline{BC}$ ☐ $\overrightarrow{BC}$

CHALLENGE How many line segments can be formed using these 4 points?

Line And Ray

Line – A line has no end points and can be extended in both directions. AB is a line, the symbol for the line is: $\overleftrightarrow{AB}$

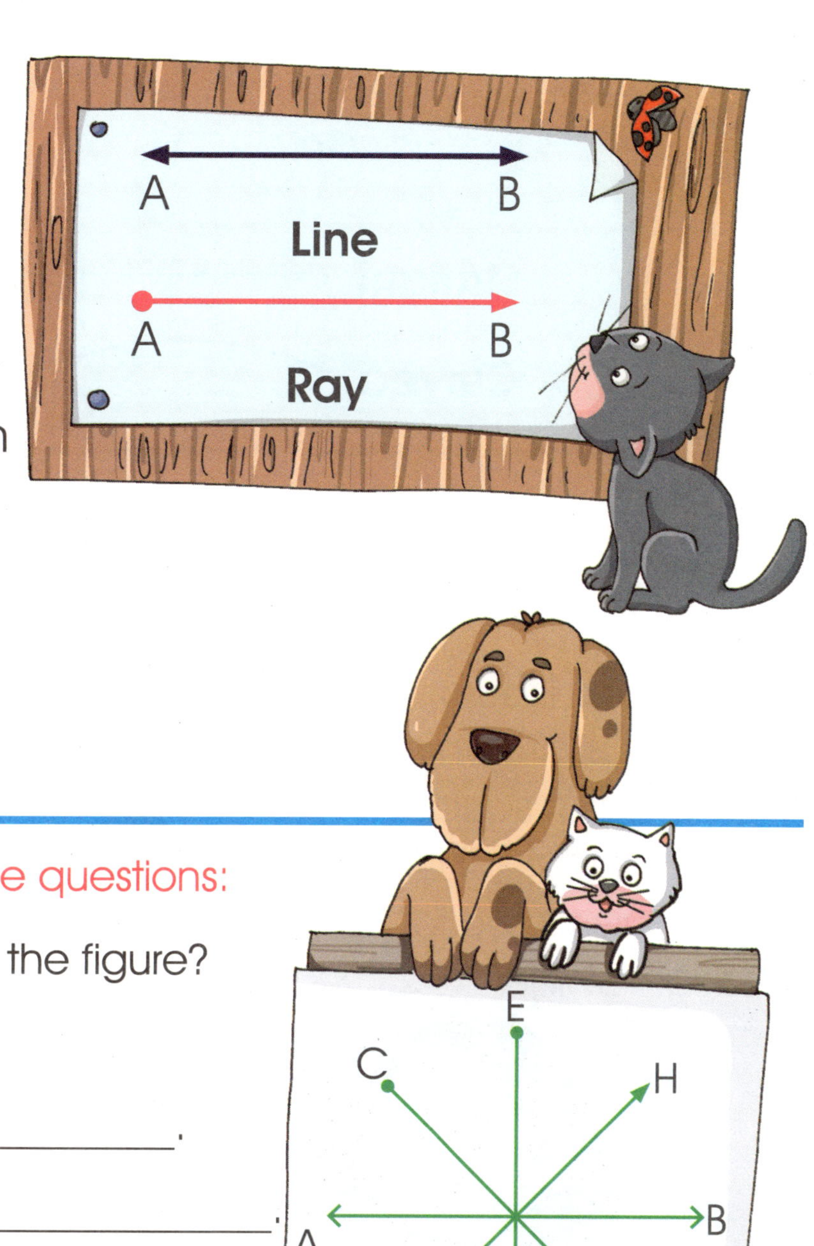

Ray – A ray has only one end point and can be extended in the direction that is opposite to the endpoint. It has no definite length. AB is a ray, with A as the initial point. It is represented as $\overrightarrow{AB}$.

Look at the picture and answer the questions:

1. How many rays can you see in the figure?

   ________________.

2. CD is an example of a ________________.
3. Name a line from the figure ________________.
4. EF is an example of a ________________.
5. What do letters C and E represent?

   ________________.

CHALLENGE Which of the following statements is false?

1. It is possible to have a line segment as a part of a line.
2. It is possible to have a line segment as a part of a ray.

Kinds Of Lines

Lines can be straight or curved.

Straight
Curved

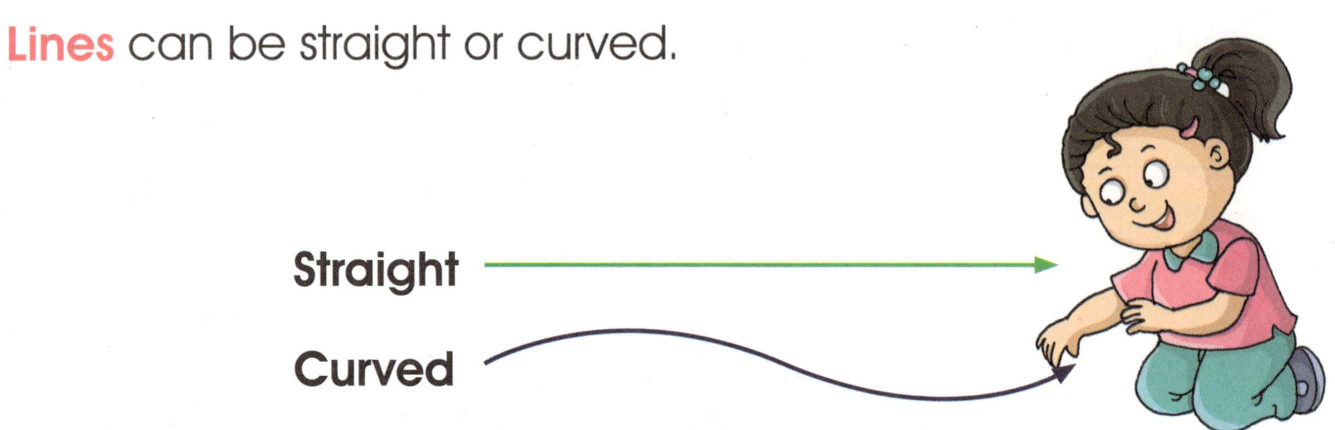

Straight lines may be drawn in different directions and are given three names:

Horizontal Lines: A line that is drawn along a flat surface from left to right or right to left is called a horizontal line.

Vertical Lines: A line that is drawn straight or upright or vertically is called a vertical line.

Slanting LInes: A line which is neither horizontal nor vertical is called a slanting or oblique line.

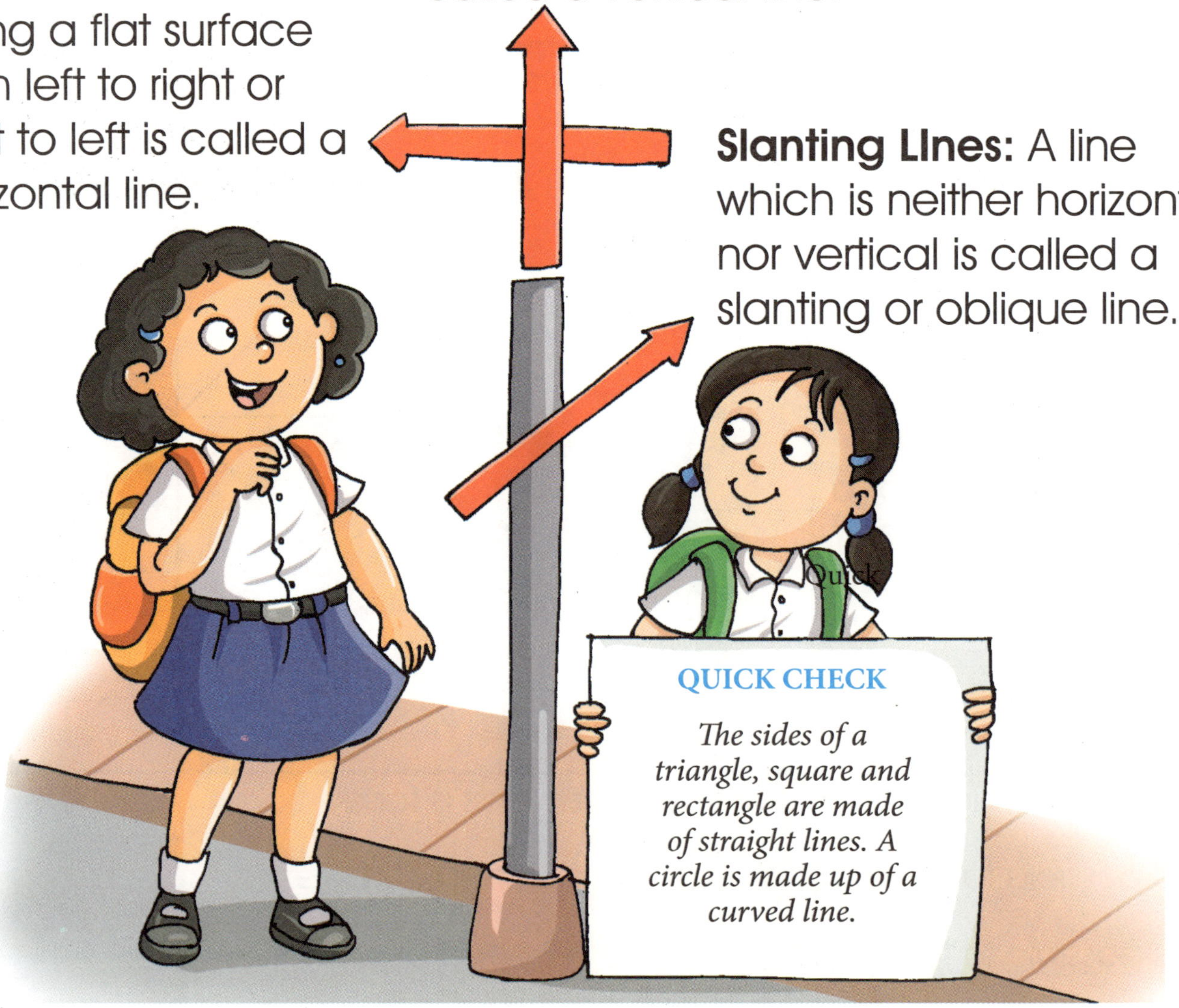

QUICK CHECK
The sides of a triangle, square and rectangle are made of straight lines. A circle is made up of a curved line.

Kinds Of Lines

Write the number for each one given in the pictures below:

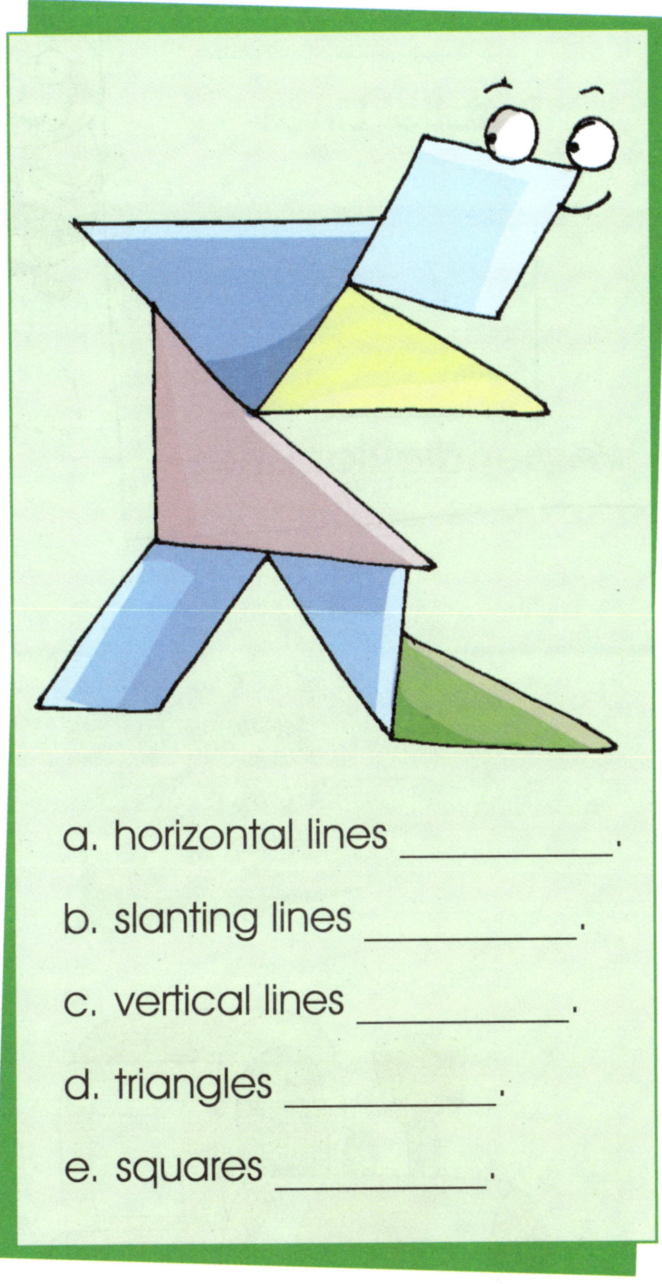

a. horizontal lines ____________.

b. slanting lines ____________.

c. vertical lines ____________.

d. triangles ____________.

e. squares ____________.

a. circles ____________.

b. triangles ____________.

c. squares ____________.

d. curves ____________.

e. slanting lines ____________.

CHALLENGE

What am I? My hands are examples of ____________ lines when it is 3 O' clock.

Kinds Of Lines

Parallel Lines – Lines that do not meet each other or do not intersect at any given point are called parallel lines.

Perpendicular Lines – Perpendicular lines are two or more lines that meet or intersect at a 90-degree angle. These 90-degree angles are also known as right angles.

What kinds of lines do these things have? parallel or perpendicular ?

a. railway track

____

b. vertical lines in a fence

____

c. crossroads

____

d. opposite window frames

____

CHALLENGE

Two lines can intersect only at one point. True or false?

Lines Of Angles

Angles – Two rays with a common end point form an angle. An angle that forms a square corner is a right angle.

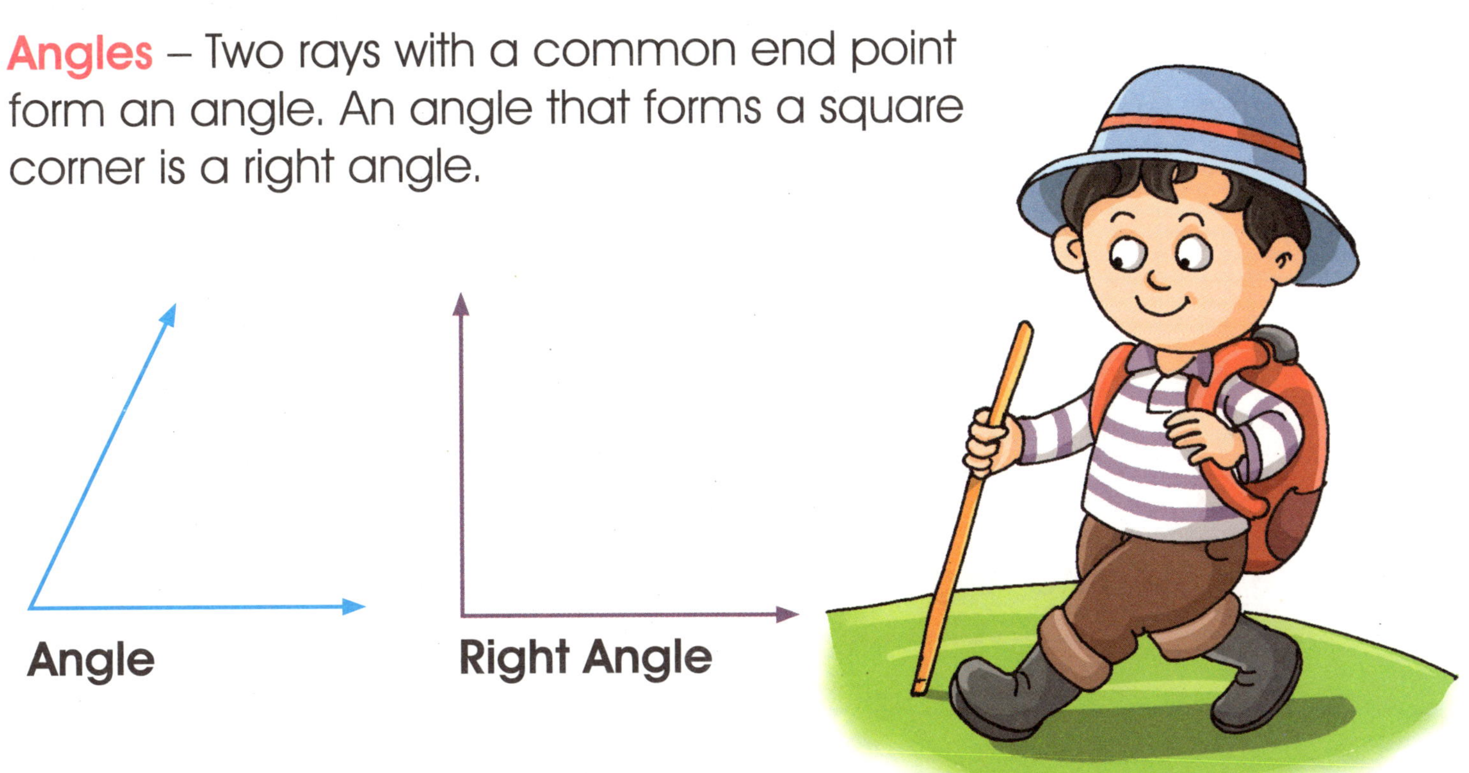

Write R for right angle, L for less than a right angle and G for greater than a right angle.

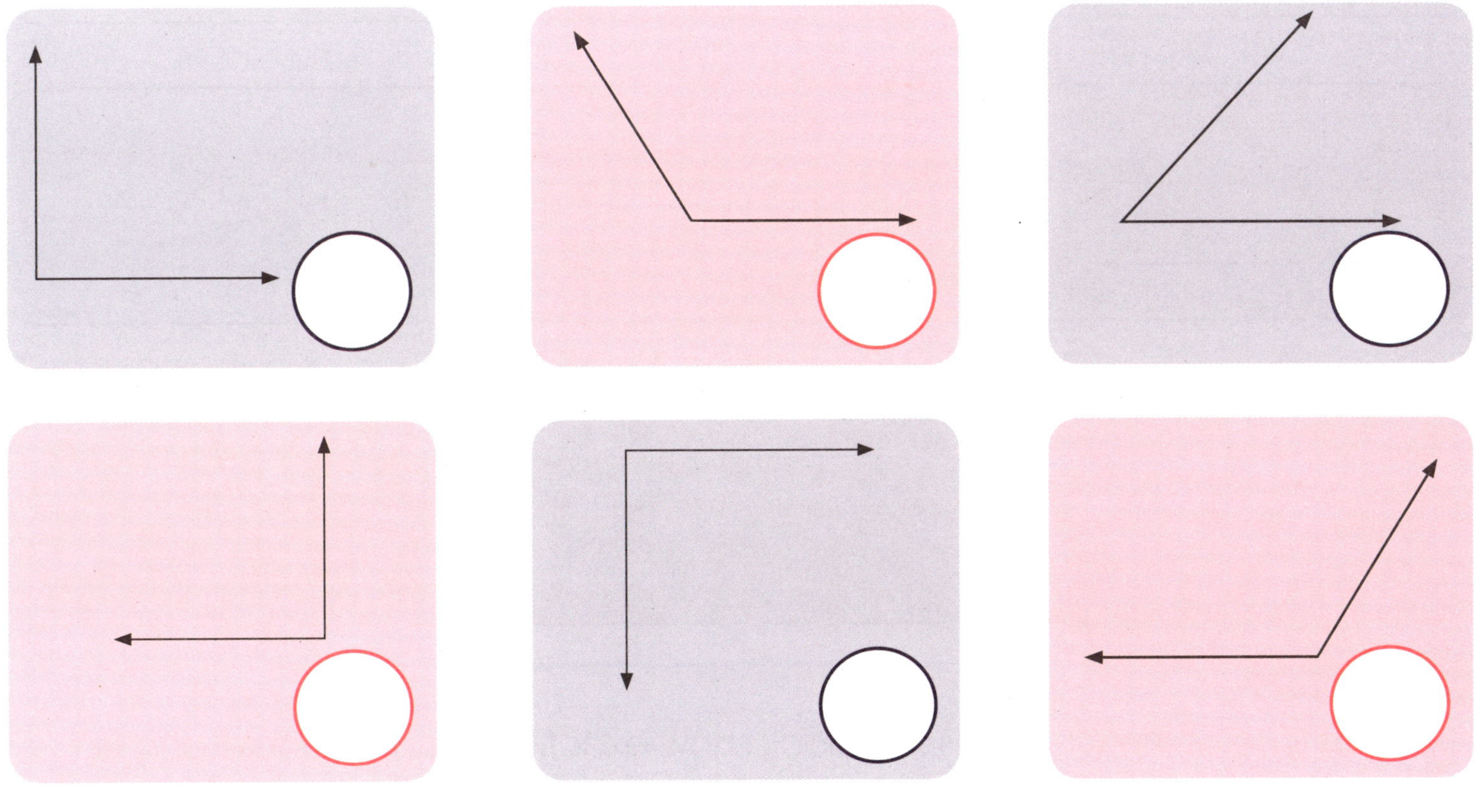

More Angles

More Angles – An angle that measures less than a right angle is an **acute angle**. An angle that measures more than a right angle is an **obtuse angle**.

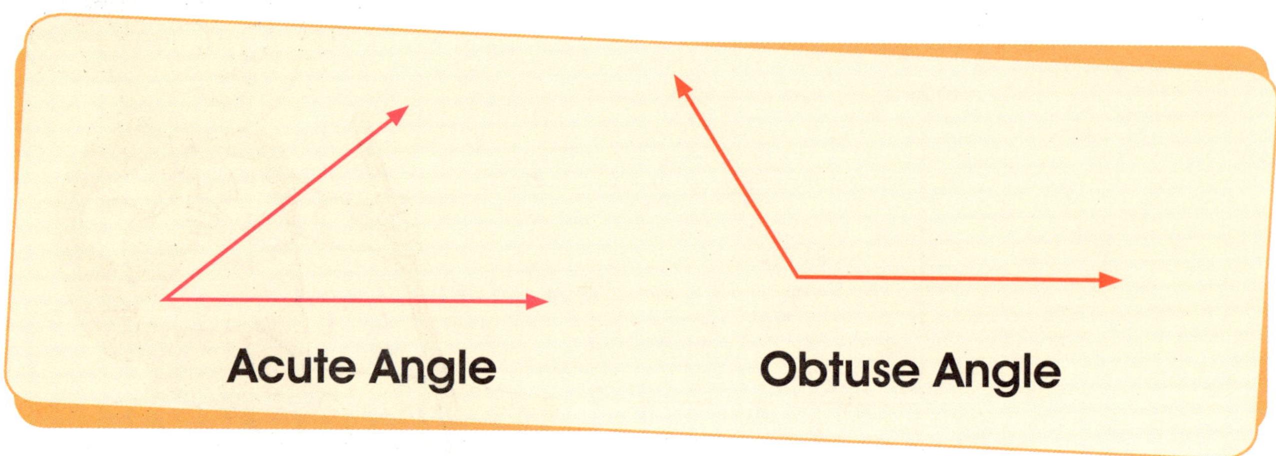

Draw a circle around the obtuse angles. Put a cross on the acute angles.

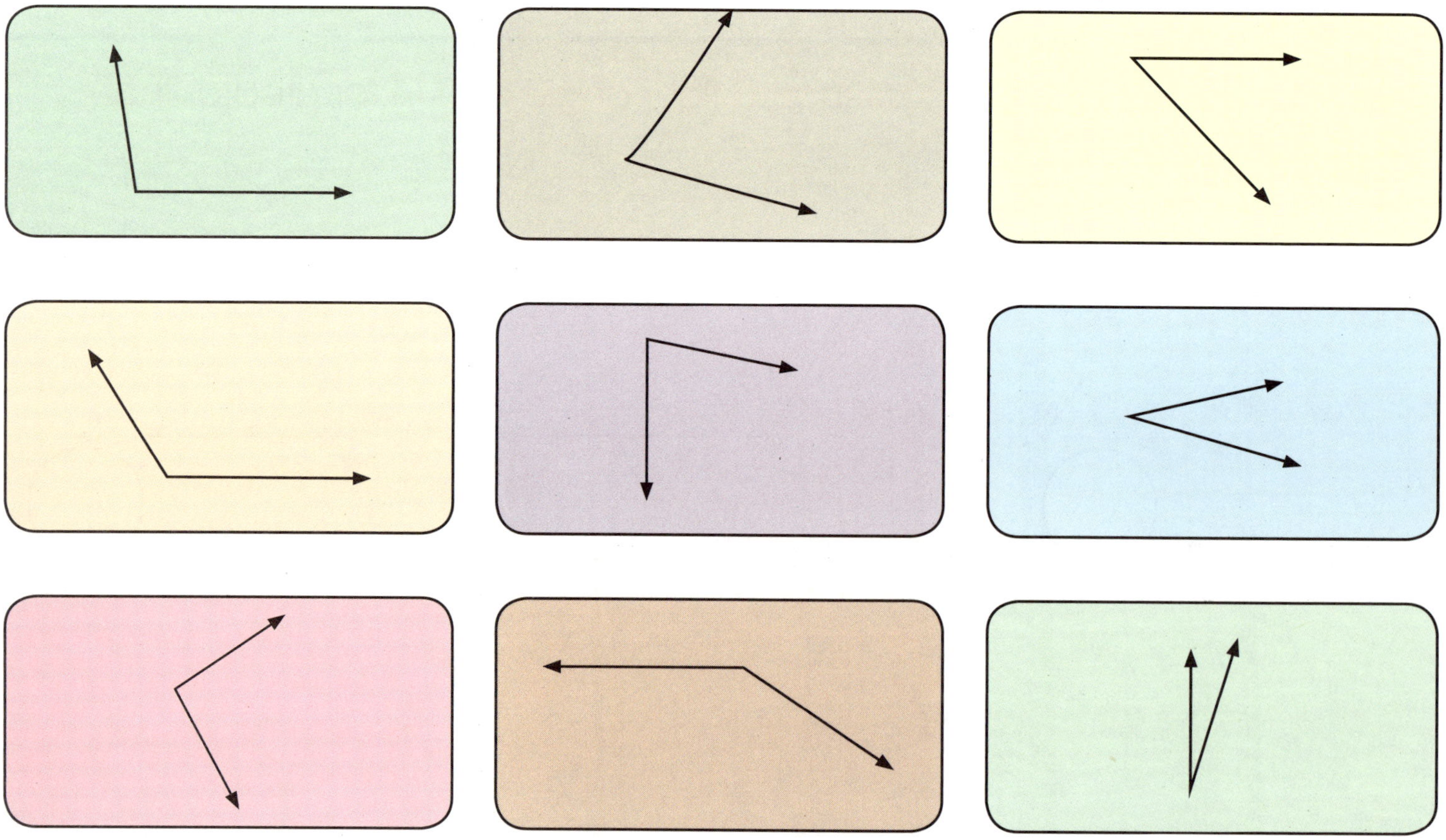

CHALLENGE

At what time of the day does the clock show exactly the same acute angles?

Angles In A Clock

Can you identify different angles shown by the hands of these clocks?
Write R for right angle, A for acute angle and O for obtuse angle.

CHALLENGE

How many times in twelve hours do the hands of a clock form a right angle?

It's A Polygon!

Polygon – A polygon is a closed plane figure that is formed by three or more line segments.

Put a tick (√) on the polygons.

CHALLENGE

Can you draw a triangle that has two same angles? Are these angles right angles?

2D Shapes

2D Shapes – A plane figure has two dimensions - width and length.

It has sides and vertices. Each side of a polygon is a line segment.

The point where two sides meet is called a vertex.

The plural of vertex is called vertices.

QUICK CHECK

2D shapes are called so because they have only two dimensions- width and length.

How many sides and vertices does each figure have? Write the number in the blocks.

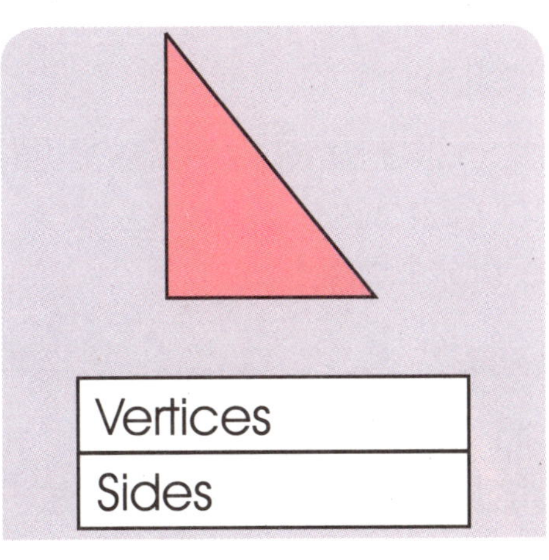

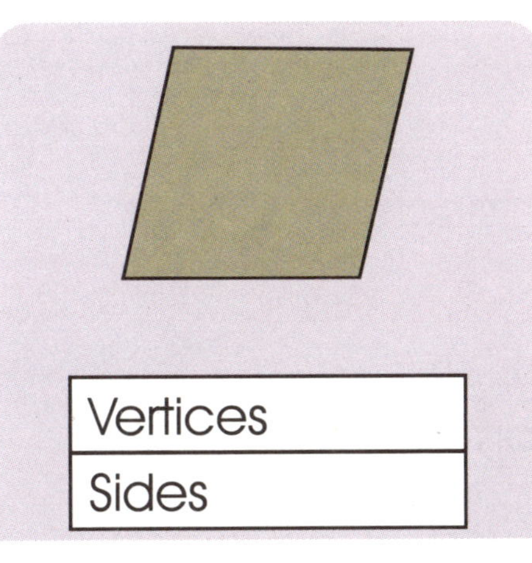

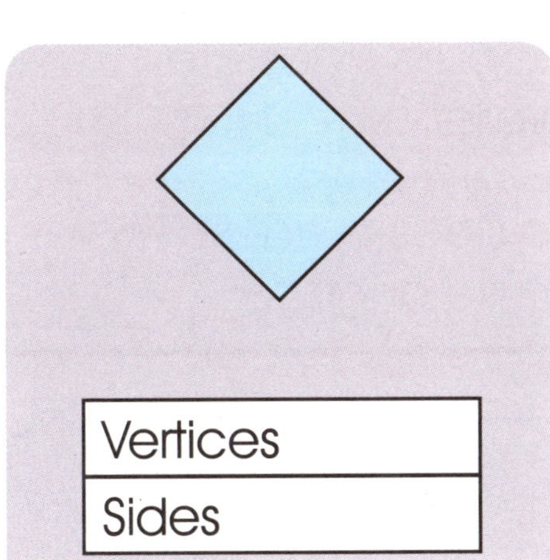

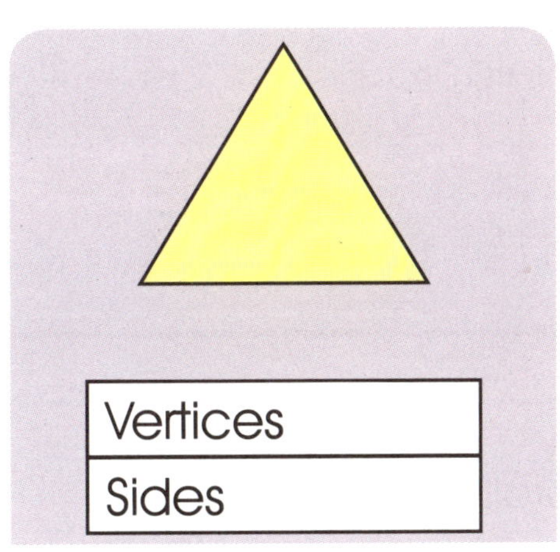

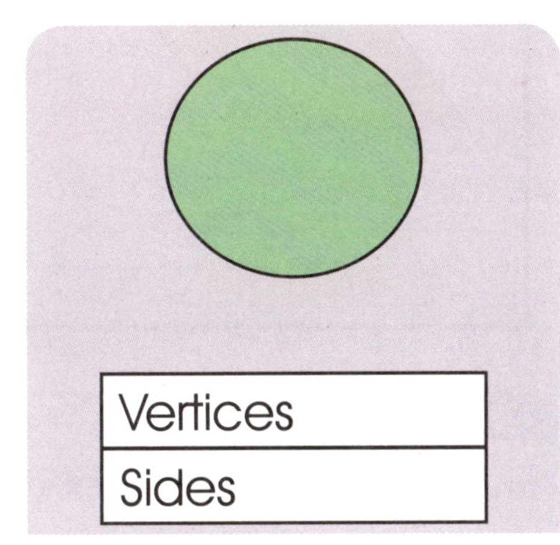

Different Polygons

Study the table to know about different polygons.

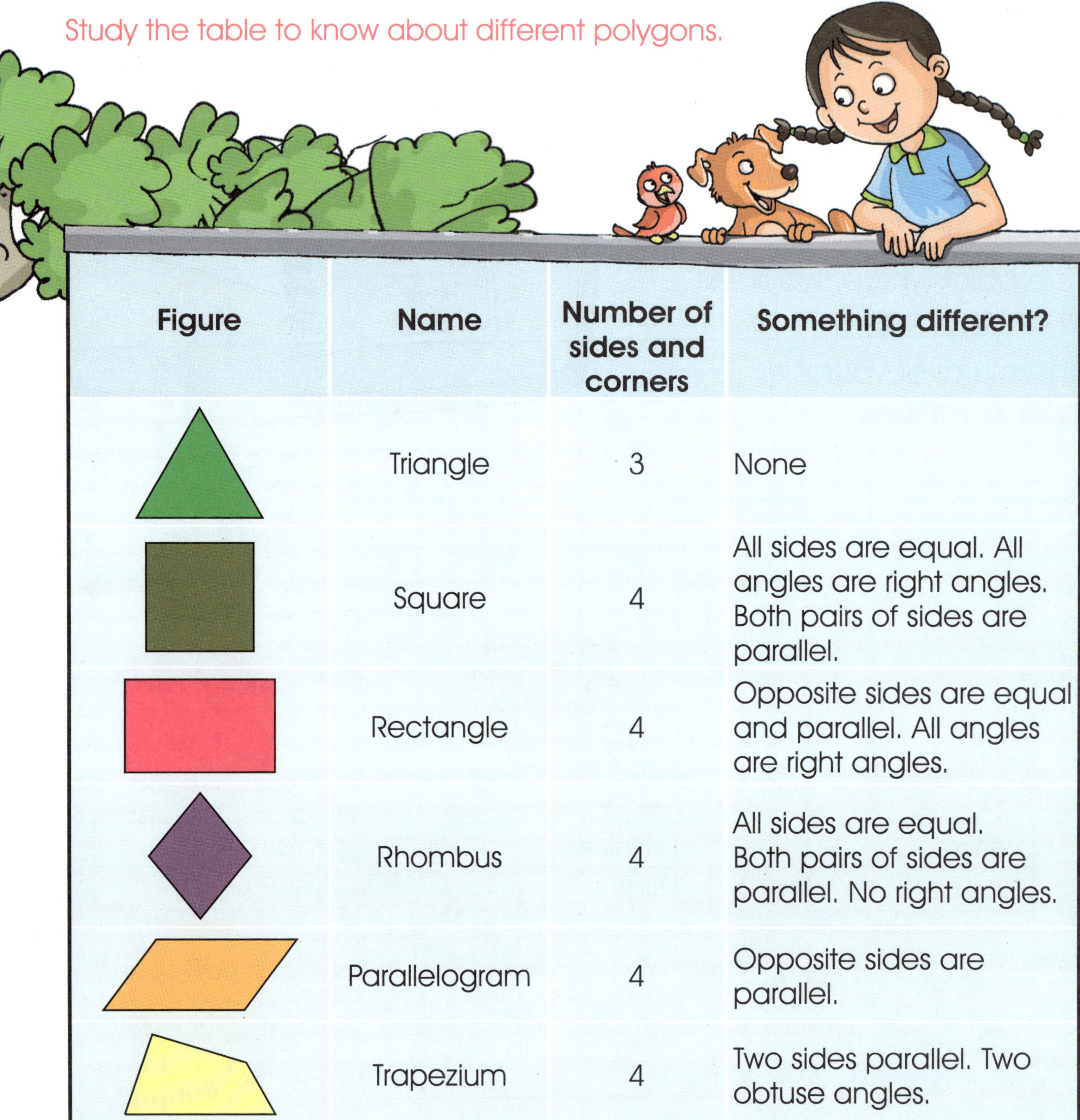

Figure	Name	Number of sides and corners	Something different?
	Triangle	3	None
	Square	4	All sides are equal. All angles are right angles. Both pairs of sides are parallel.
	Rectangle	4	Opposite sides are equal and parallel. All angles are right angles.
	Rhombus	4	All sides are equal. Both pairs of sides are parallel. No right angles.
	Parallelogram	4	Opposite sides are parallel.
	Trapezium	4	Two sides parallel. Two obtuse angles.

CHALLENGE

How are a rhombus and parallelogram similar?

Guess The Polygon!

The room is all messed up. Read the clues and find the objects that match the shapes. Number them.

1. A polygon with all right angles and all sides equal.
2. A polygon with only one pair of parallel sides.
3. A polygon with six sides.
4. A polygon with opposite sides equal.

CHALLENGE How many triangles can you draw from the given polygon?

3D Shapes

3D Shapes – A 3D shape has three dimensions- width, height and length. It has faces, edges and vertices.

Face is the flat surface of a 3D shape.

An edge is where two faces of a 3D shape meet.

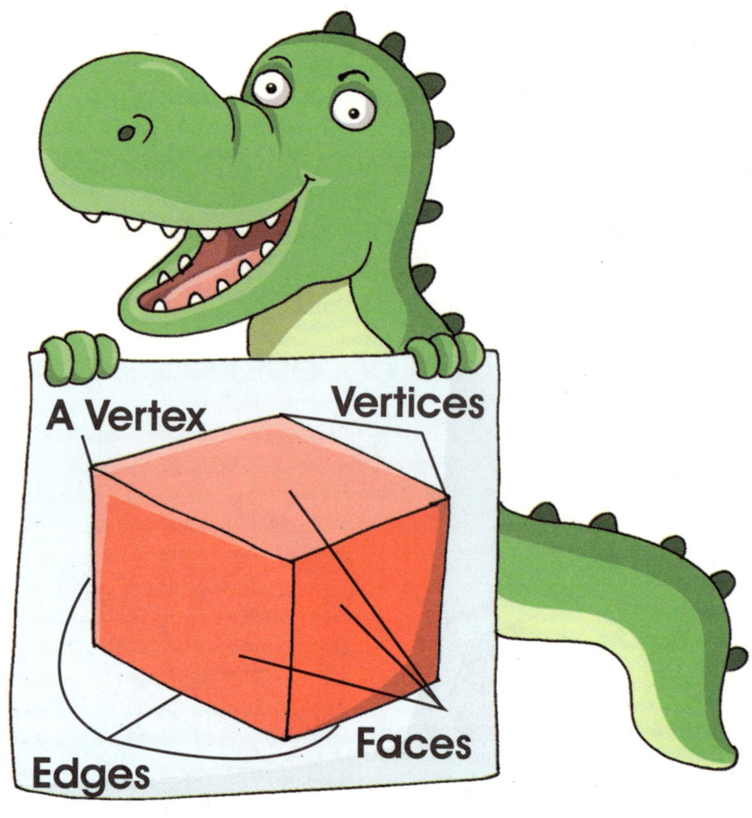

Which of the following are 3D figures? Circle them.

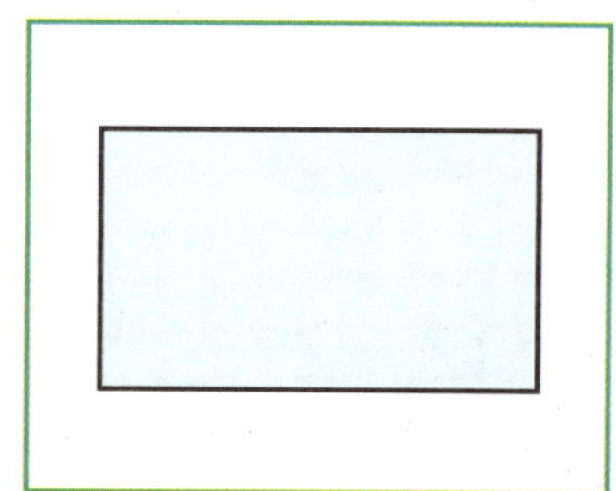  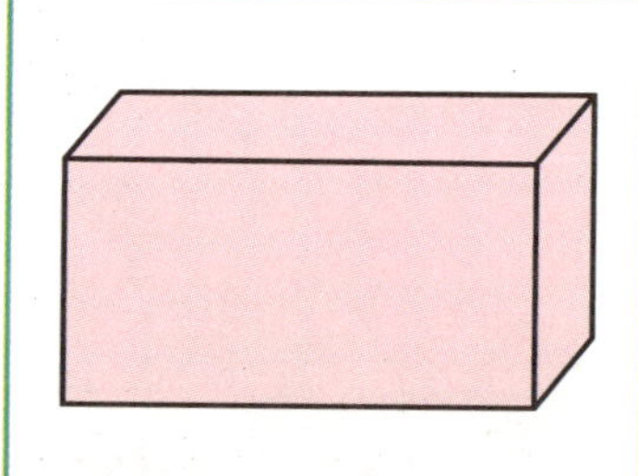 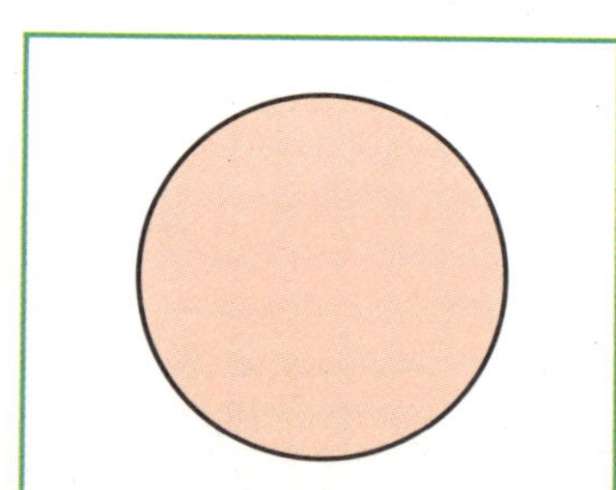

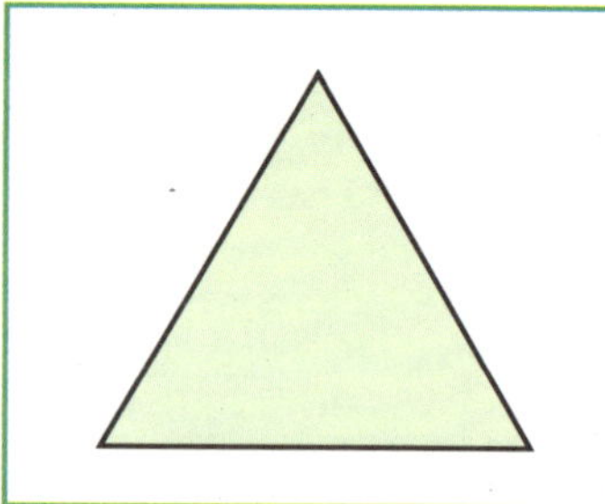  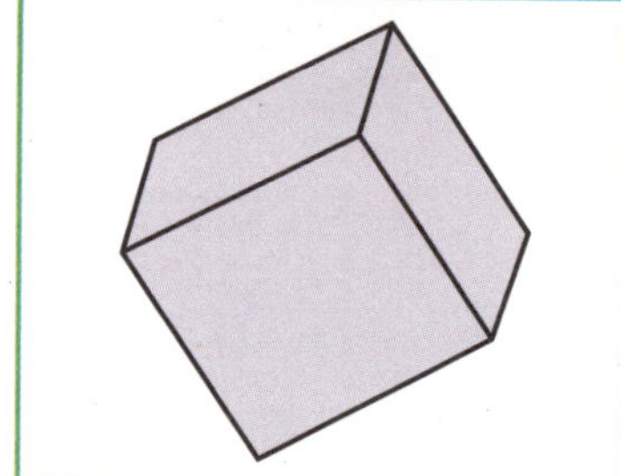 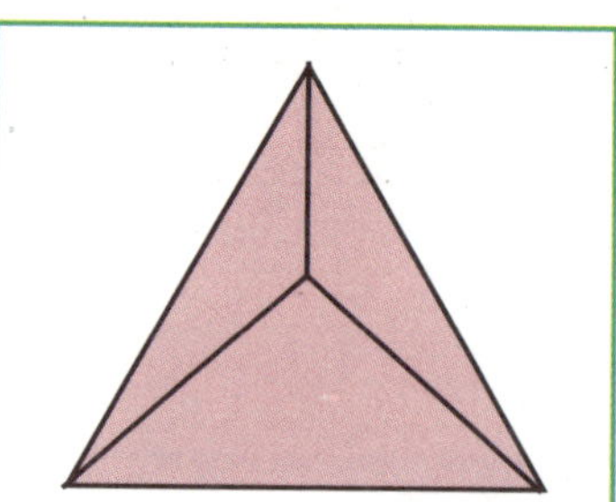

CHALLENGE

How many faces does a football have?

Exploring Different 3D Shapes

The table tells you about properties of some 3D shapes.

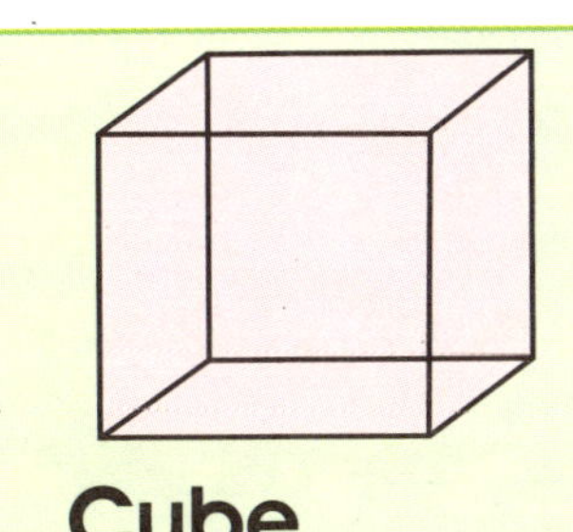
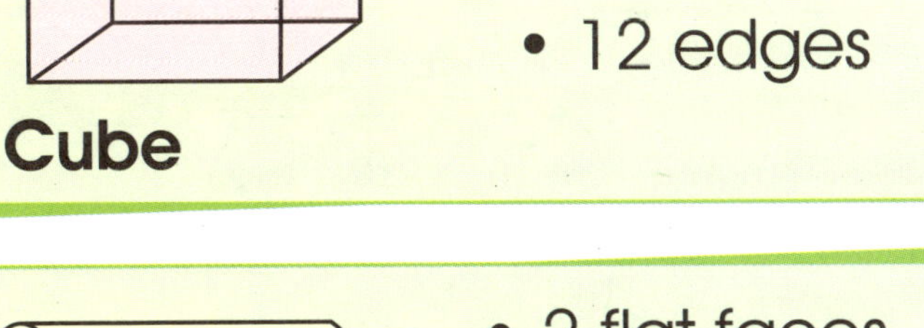

Cube

- 6 faces
- 8 vertices
- 12 edges

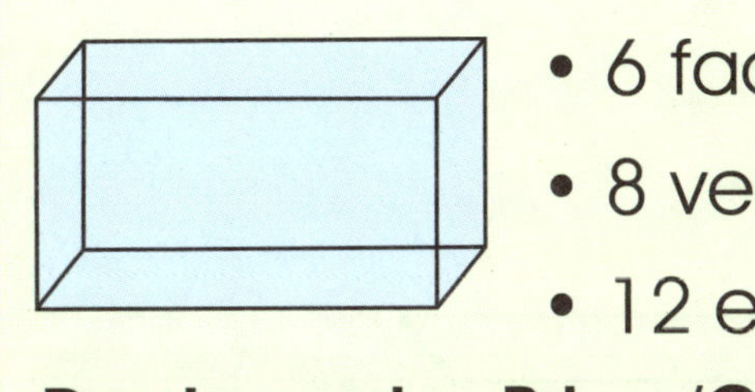

Rectangular Prism/Cuboid

- 6 faces
- 8 vertices
- 12 edges

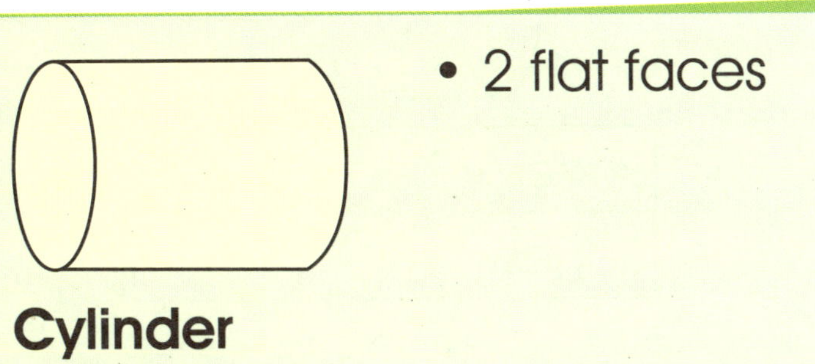

Cylinder

- 2 flat faces

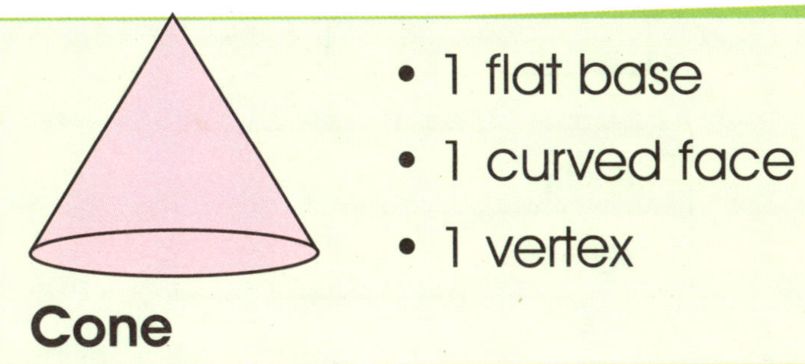

Cone

- 1 flat base
- 1 curved face
- 1 vertex

Sphere

- no edges
- no vertices

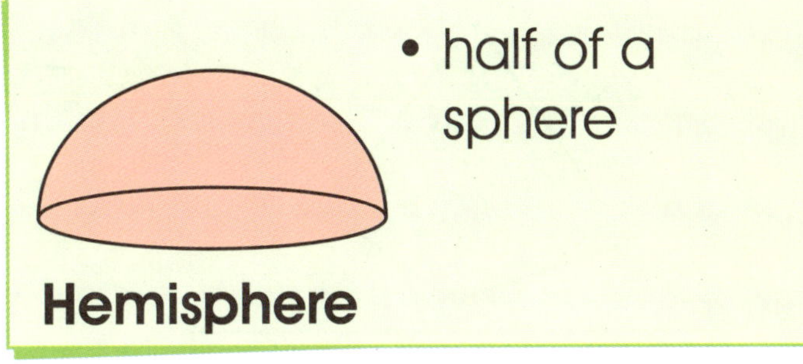

Hemisphere

- half of a sphere

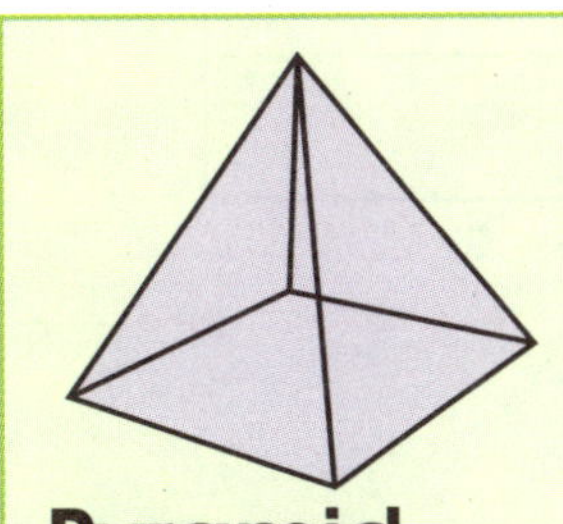

Pyramid

- flat base
- faces slope inwards

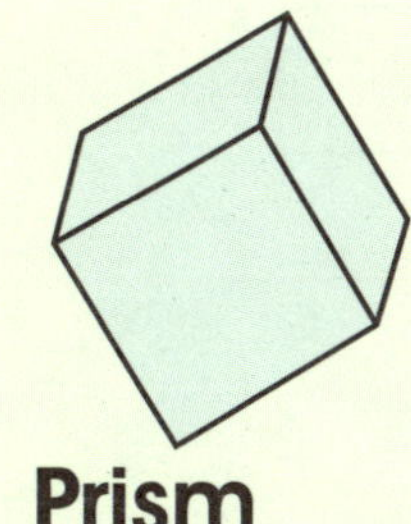

Prism

- Two opposite faces are same
- Can be triangular, pentagonal, hexagonal and more

Pyramids are named according to the shape of their base.

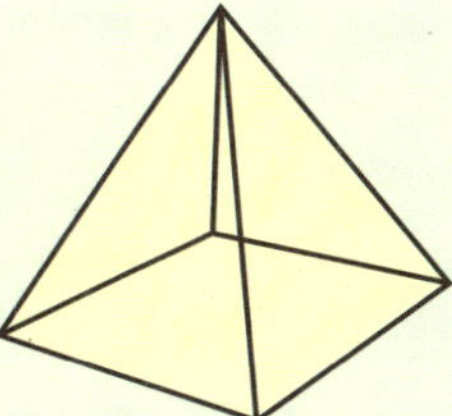

Square Pyramid

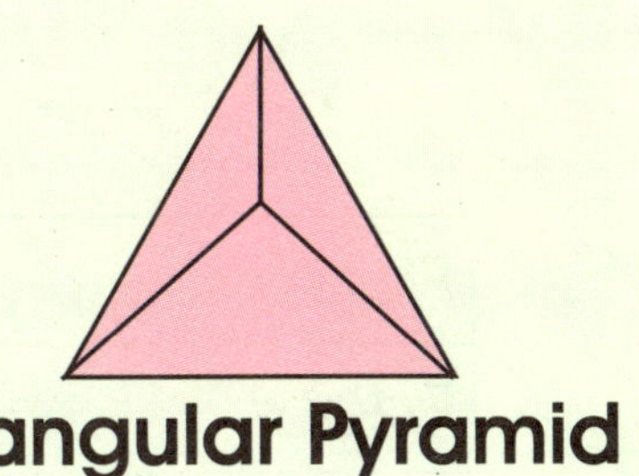

Triangular Pyramid

Faces And Edges!

How many faces and edges does each figure have? Write the number.

QUICK CHECK
3D shapes are called so because they have three dimensions- width, height and length.

Faces	
Edges	

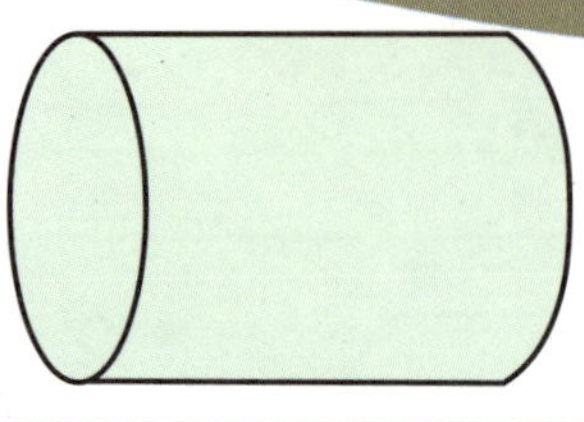

Faces	
Edges	

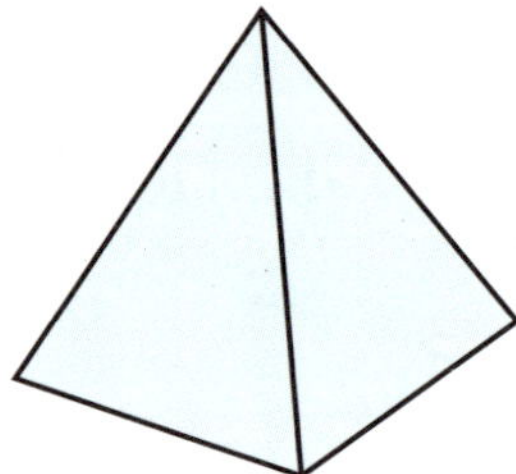

Faces	
Edges	

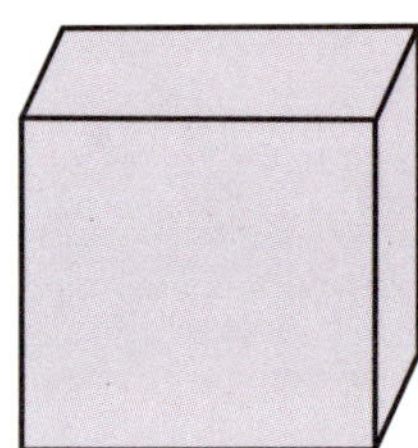

Faces	
Edges	

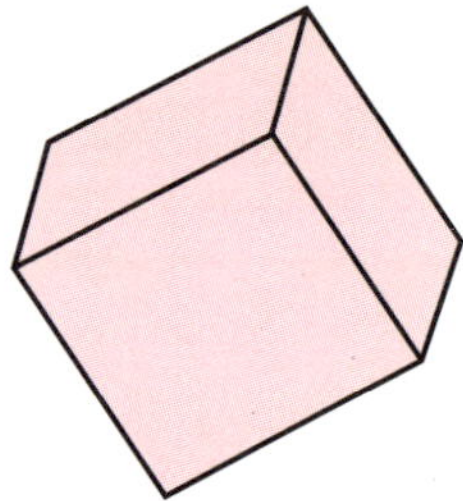

Faces	
Edges	

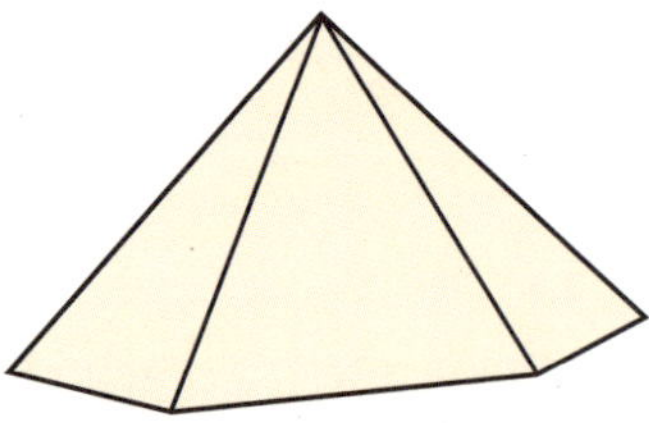

Faces	
Edges	

Nets Of 3D Shapes

Nets of 3D Shapes – The net of a 3D shape is what the shape looks like when it is opened up and spread out as a two dimensional or 2D figure.

Identifying Nets

Tick (✓) the box with the correct net for each 3D shape.

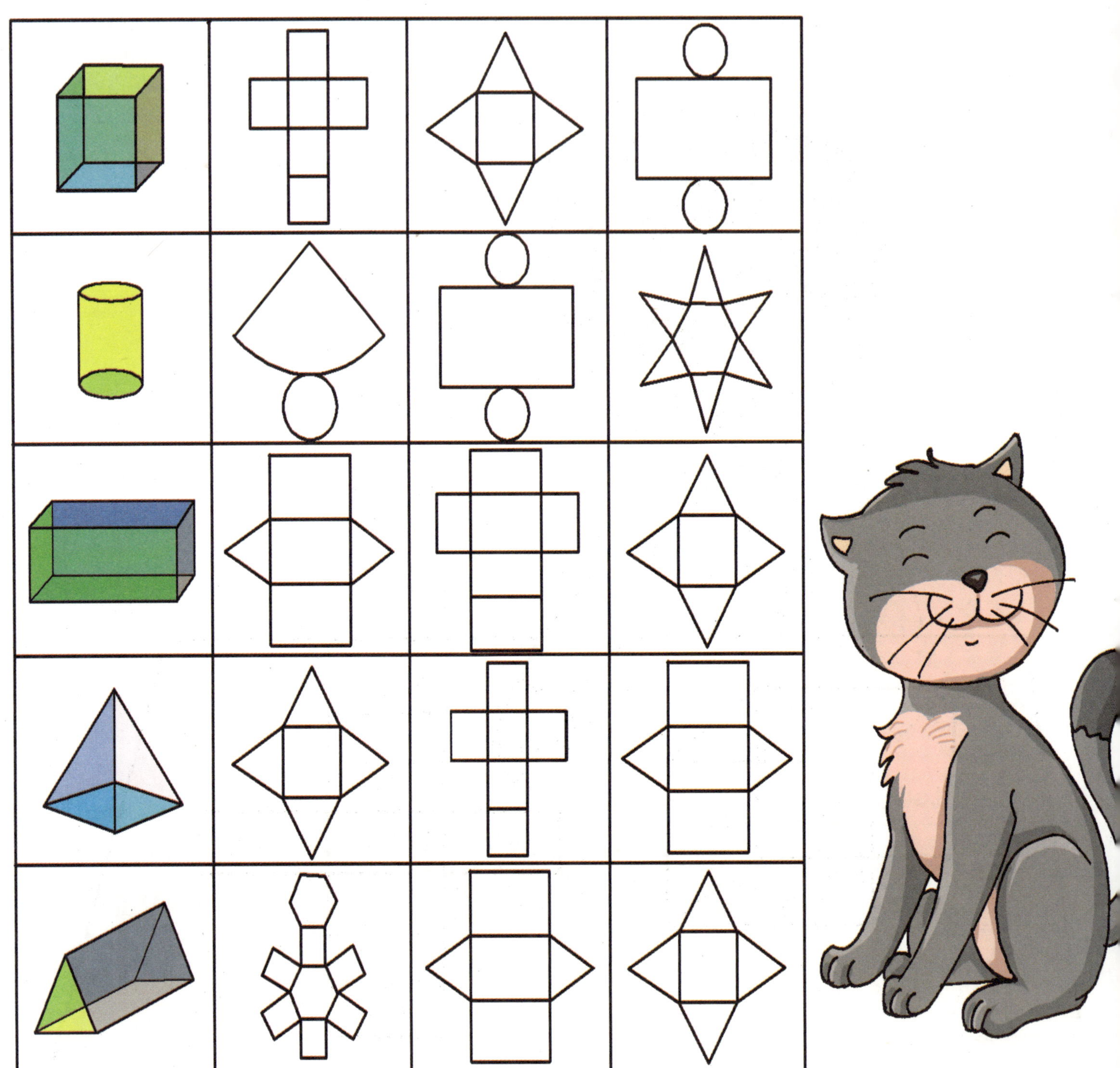

CHALLENGE

Is it possible to draw the net of a sphere? Give it a try and share your findings here.

Symmetry

Symmetry – It is when a shape looks identical to its original shape after being flipped or turned. Symmetry is thus a mirror image.

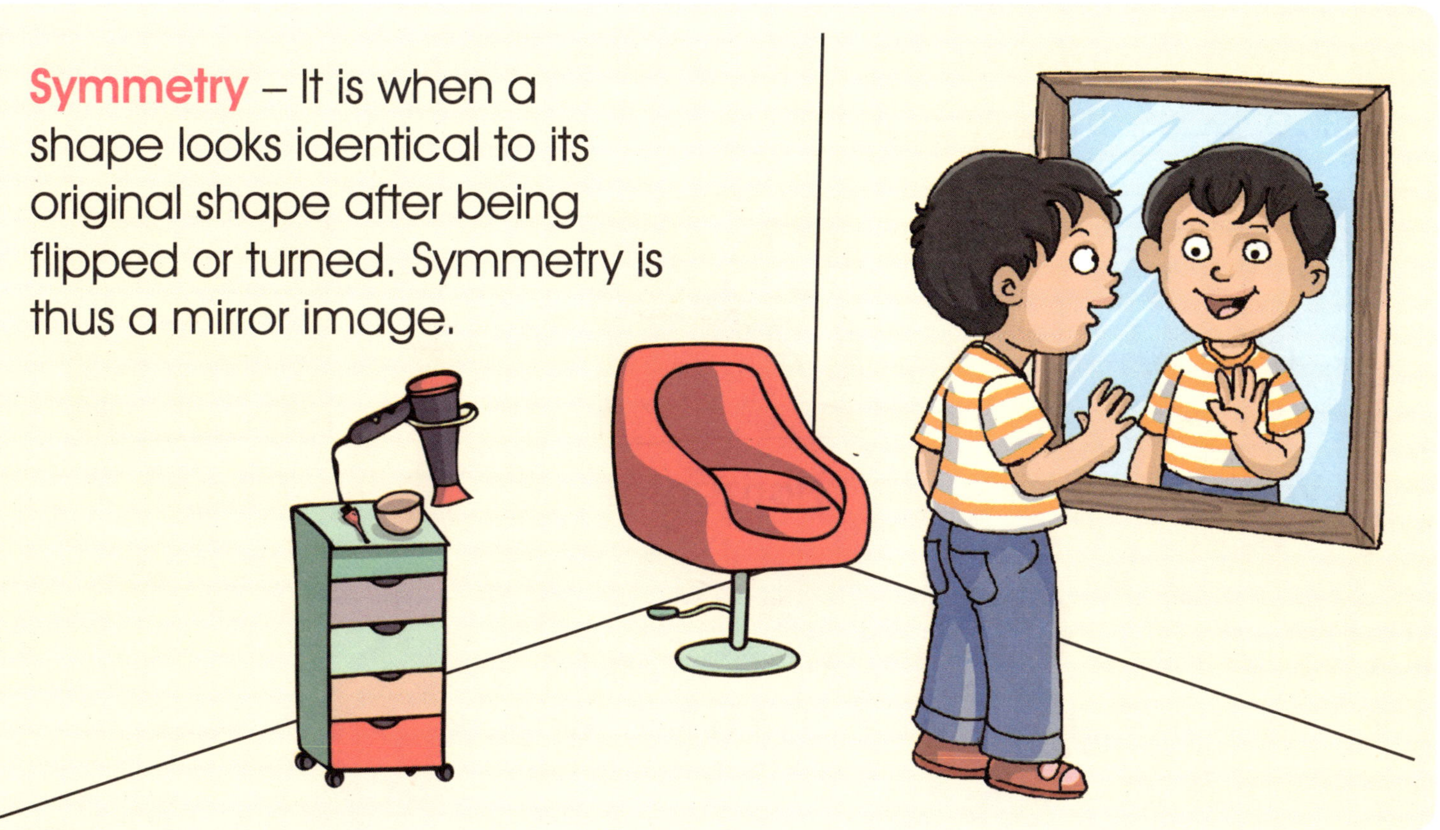

Which two images mirror each other? Circle them.

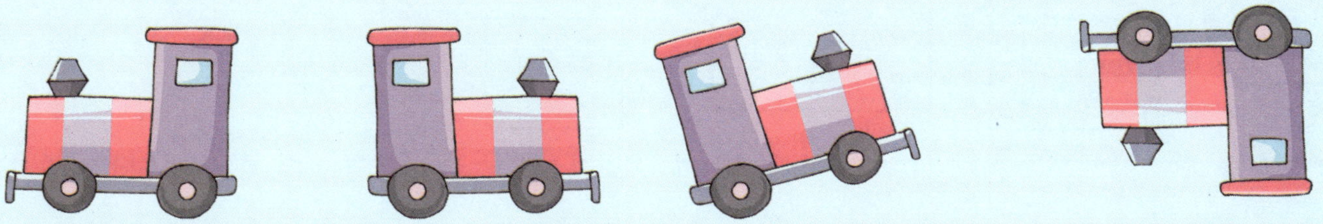

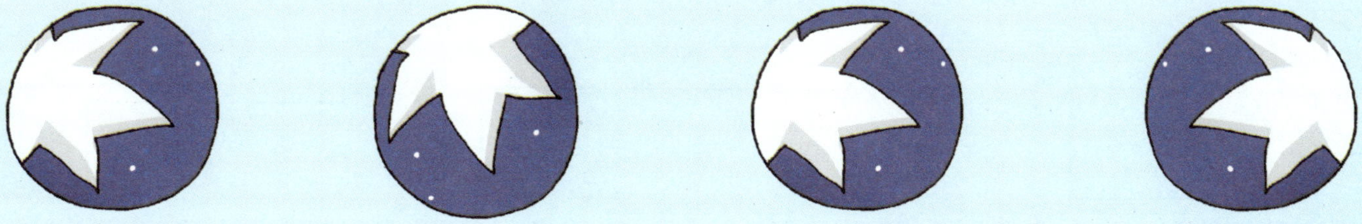

Line Of Symmetry

Line of Symmetry – The line of symmetry divides a shape into two identical parts. The line can be vertical, horizontal or diagonal.

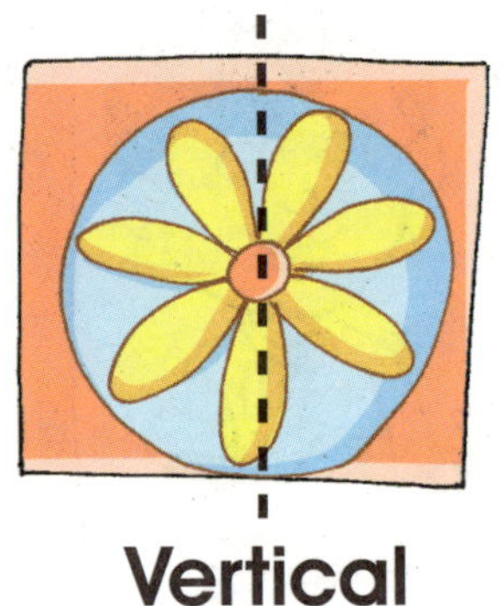

Vertical

Horizontal

Diagonal

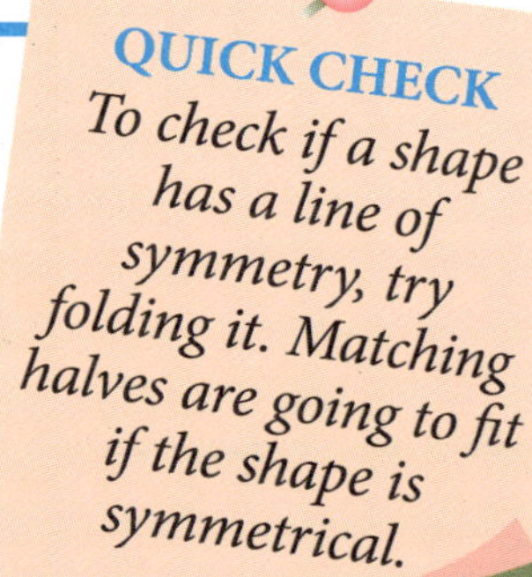

Tick (✓) the shapes that have line of symmetry.
Write V for vertical, H for horizontal and D for diagonal line of symmetry.

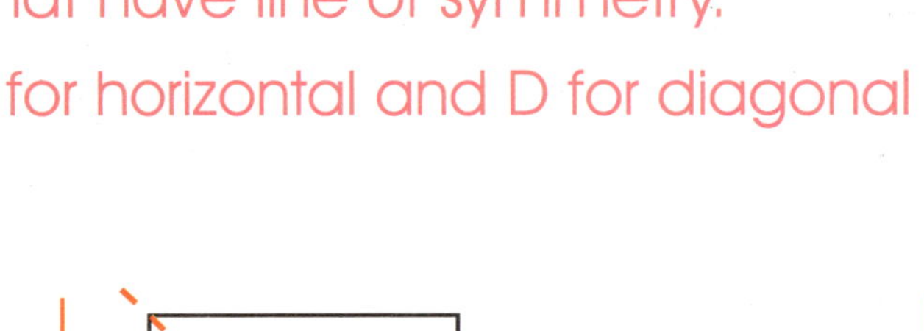

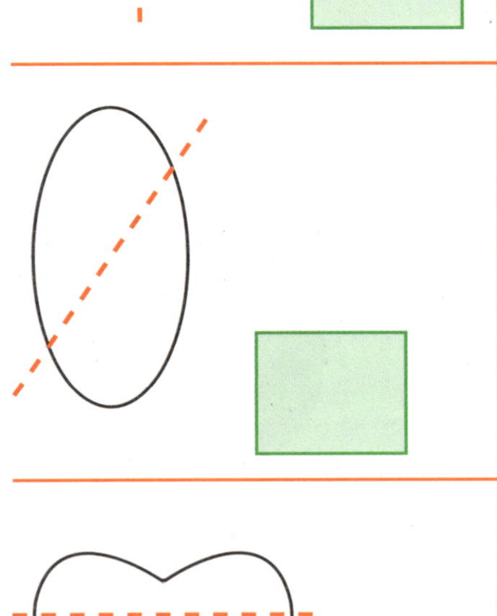

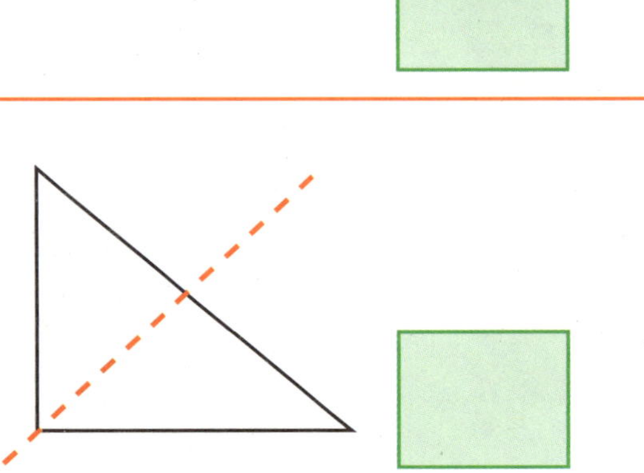

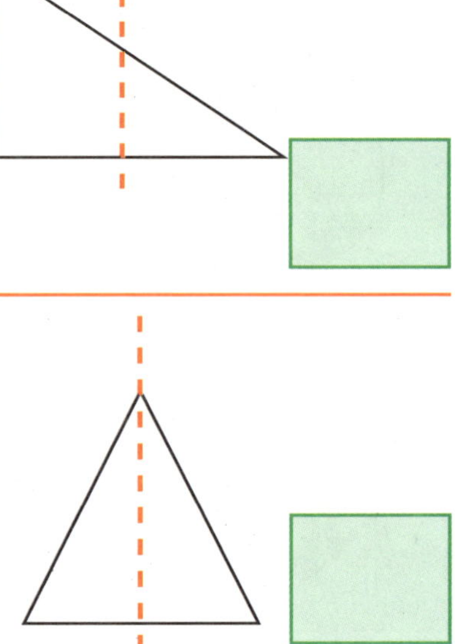

Half Yours, Half Mine!

Can you draw a line of symmetry to divide these shapes into equal halves? Give it a try!

Line Of Symmetry

Line of Symmetry – You can fold some shapes in two different ways so that the sides meet. Such shapes have more than one line of symmetry. The shape given below has two different lines of symmetry.

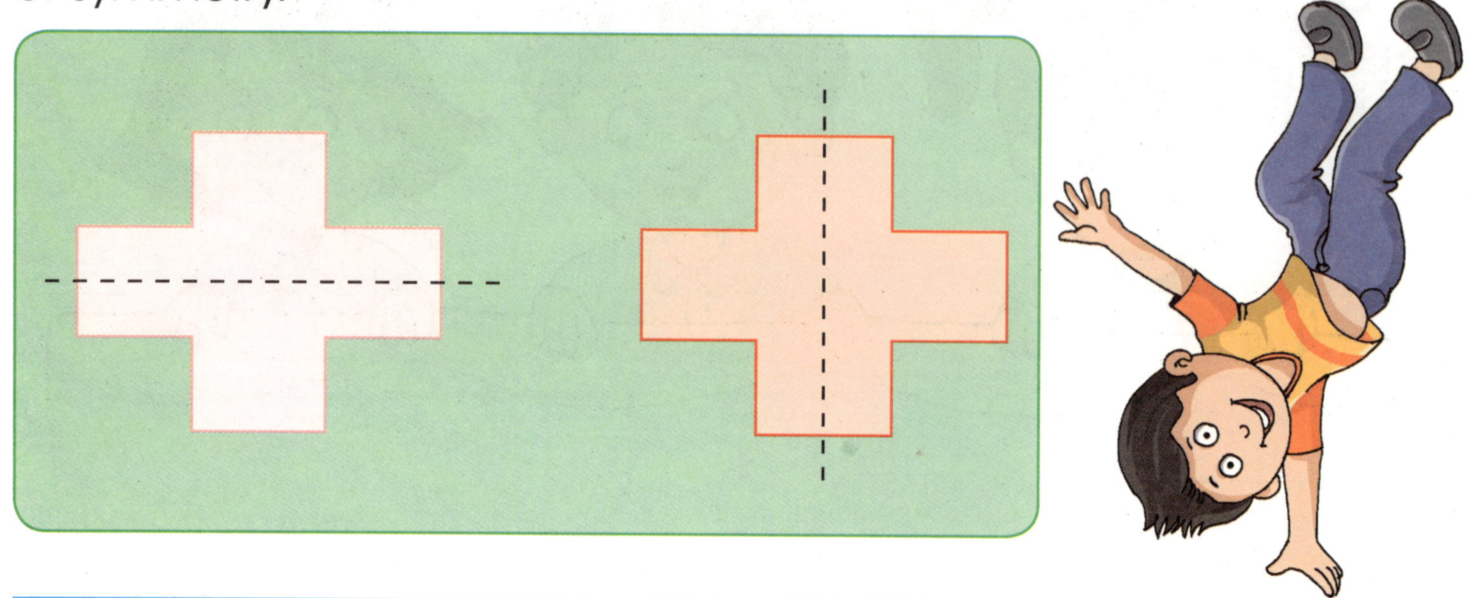

Draw as many lines of symmetry as you can for these shapes. Write the number of lines you draw in the box.

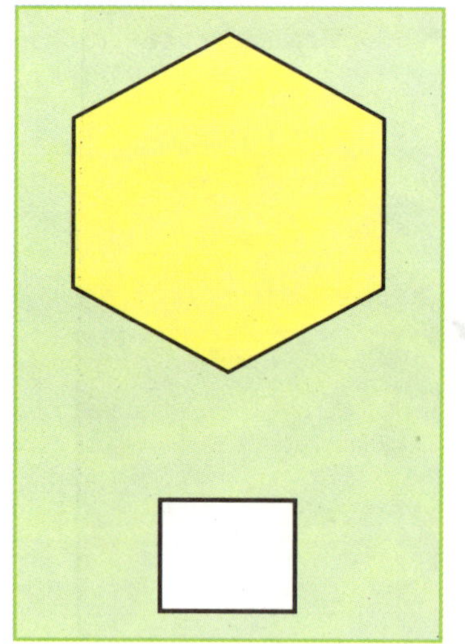
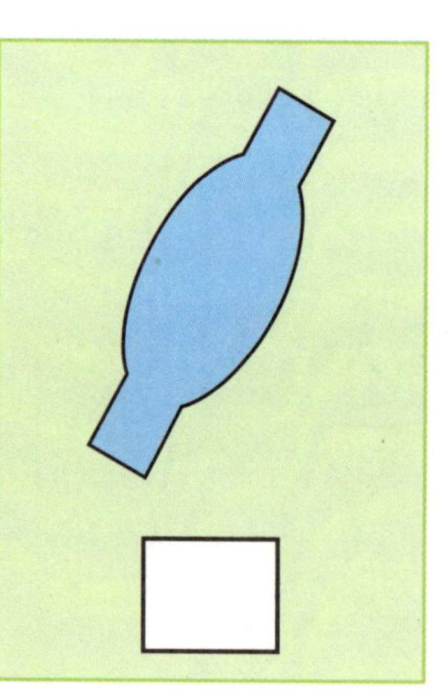
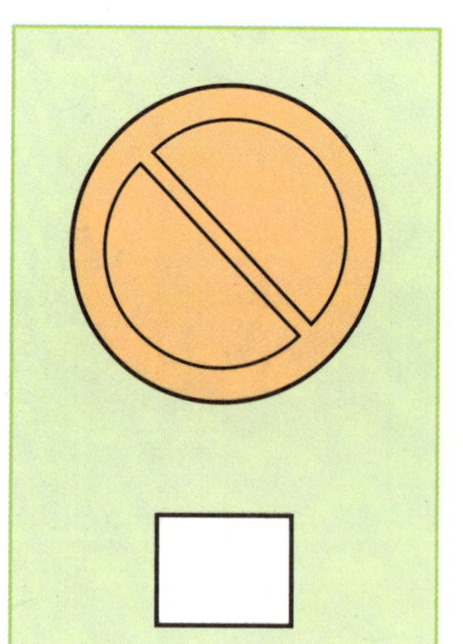
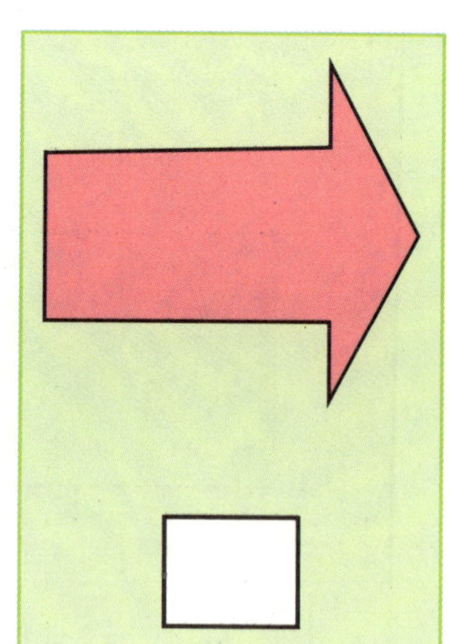

CHALLENGE Do the flags have any lines of symmetry? If so, how many?

Where Is The Other Half?

Point – Complete the second half of each picture to show symmetry.

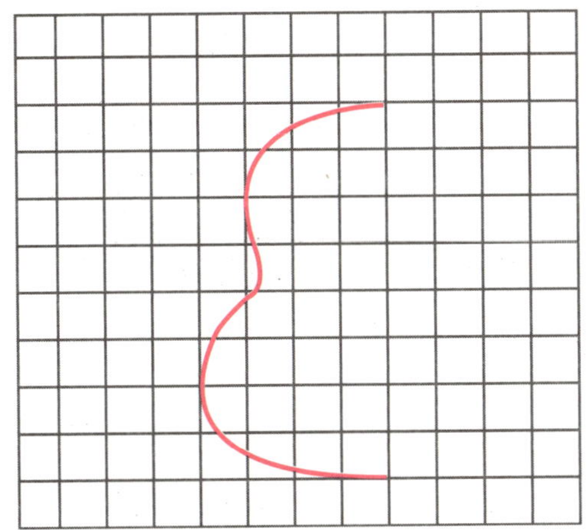

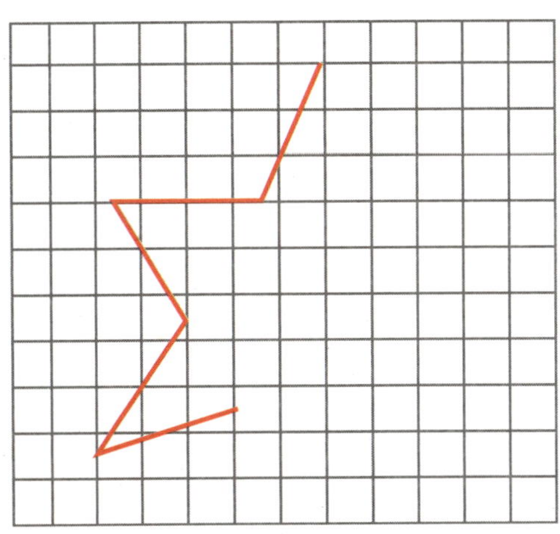

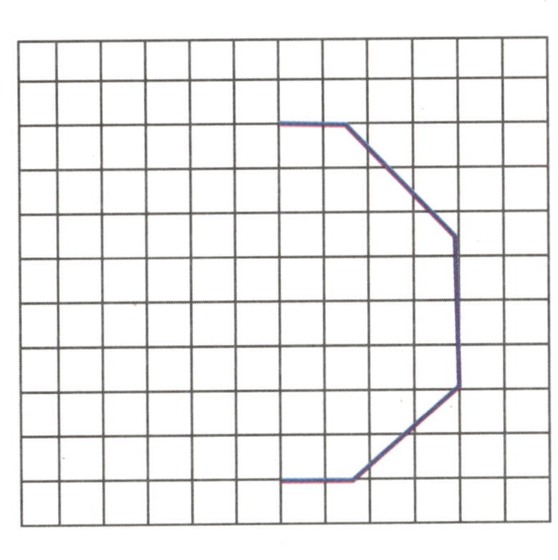

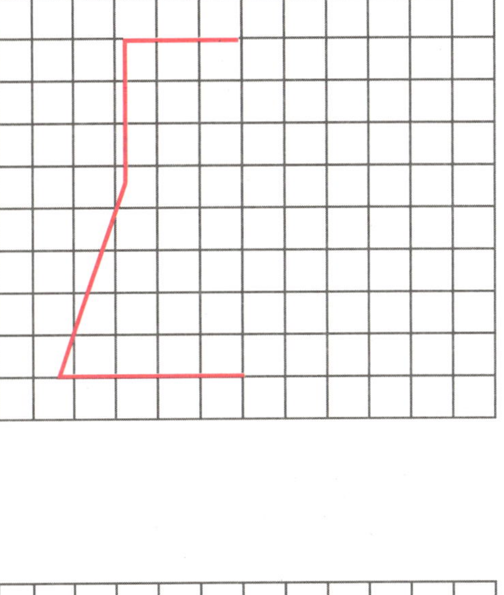

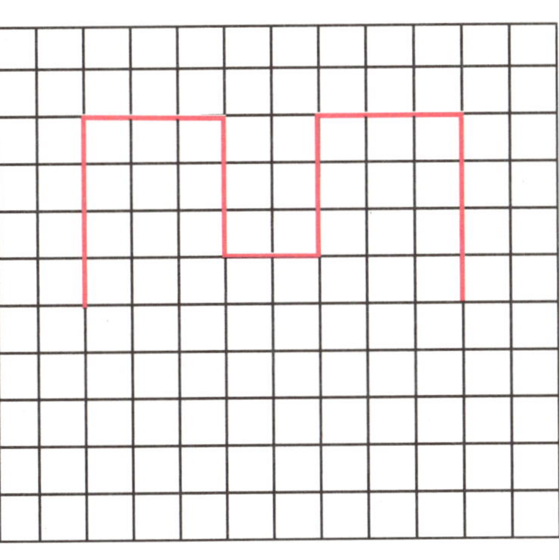

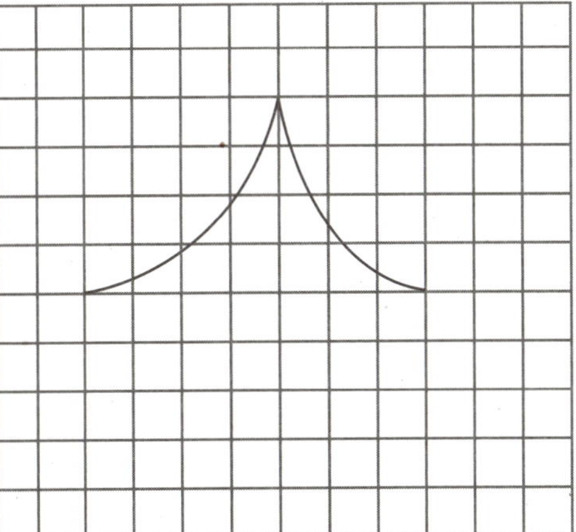

Symmetry In Letters Of Alphabet

Draw lines of symmetry for the letters of the English alphabet given below.

Sort the letters into the correct columns.

No line of symmetry	1 line of symmetry	2 lines of symmetry

CHALLENGE

Which letters in the English alphabet do not change in their mirror image? Write them here.

Transforming Shapes

You can transform a figure in three ways:

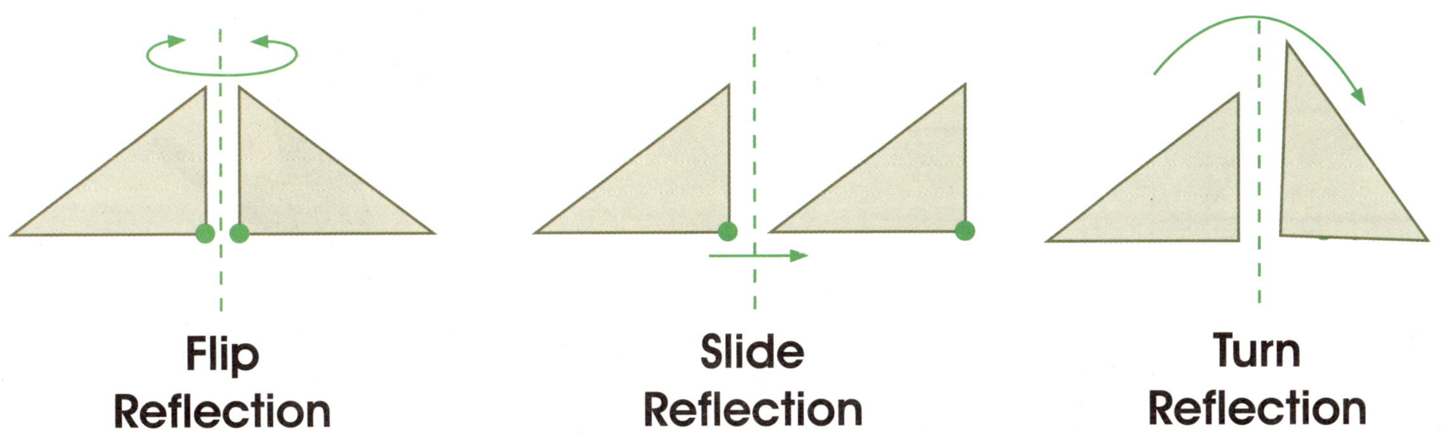

Put a tick (✓) on the figures that show flip.

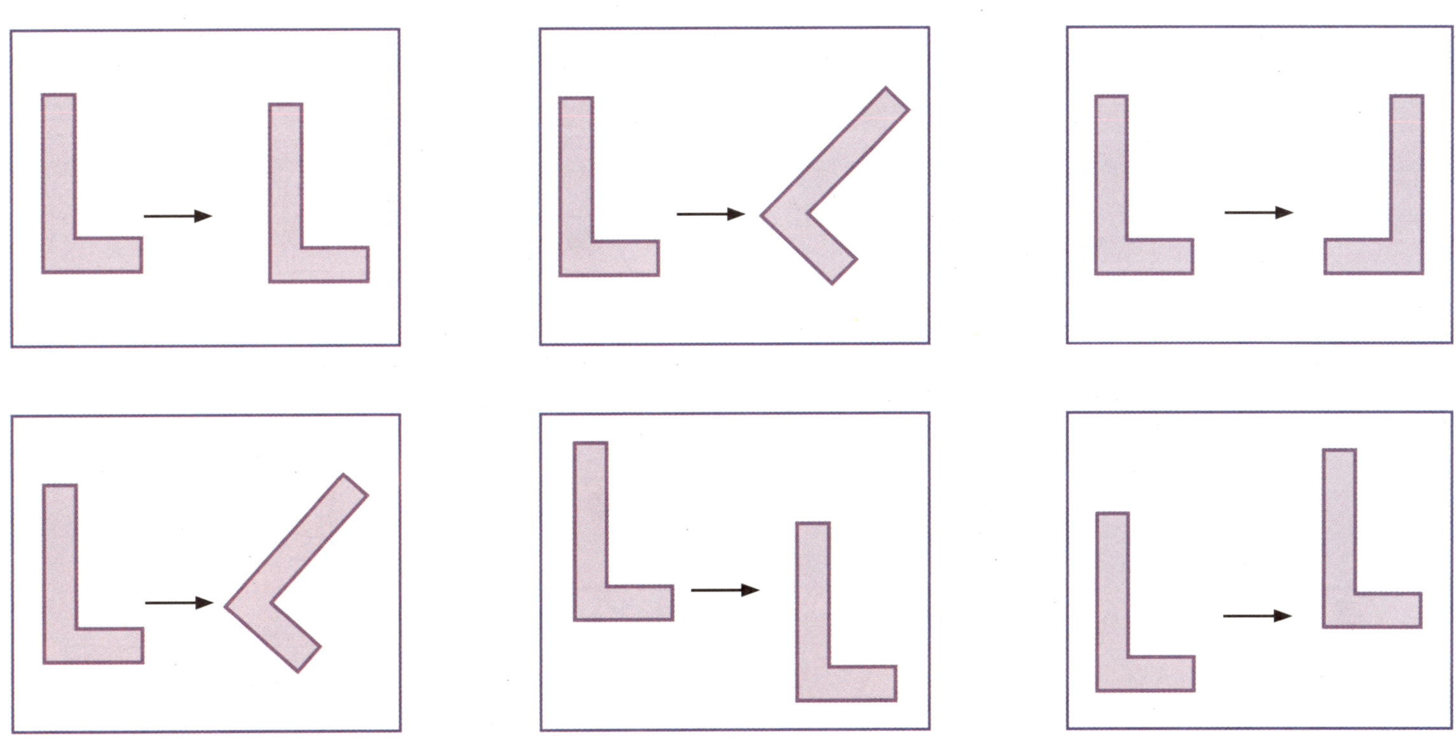

CHALLENGE The figure here shows the left side of the time shown by a digital clock. Flip the numbers and write them on the right side of the symmetry line. What time does the digital clock show?

Transforming Shapes

Put a tick (✓) on the figures that show slide.

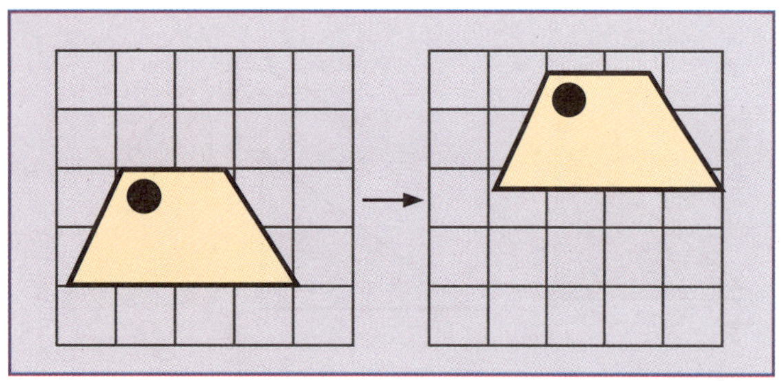

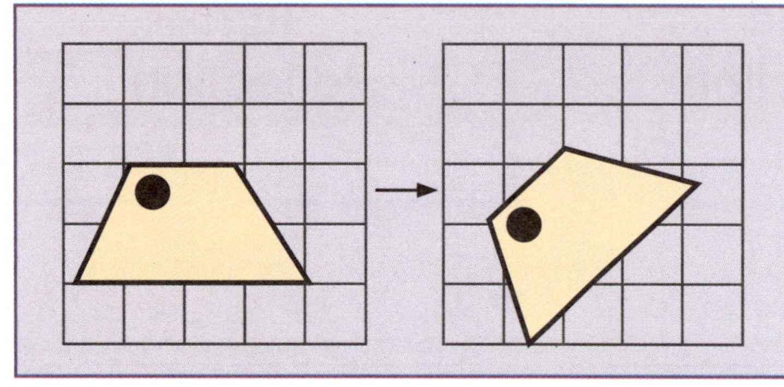

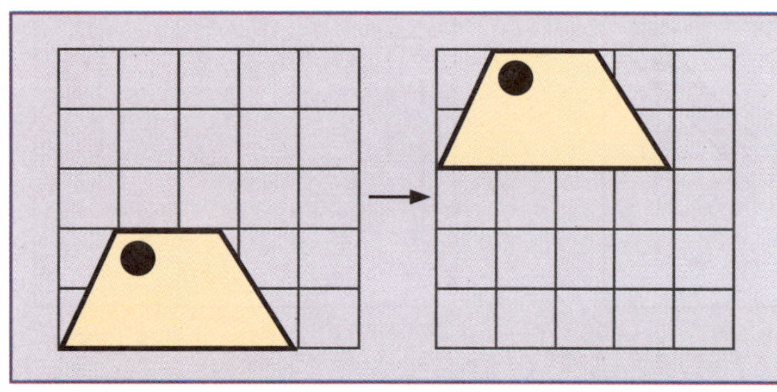

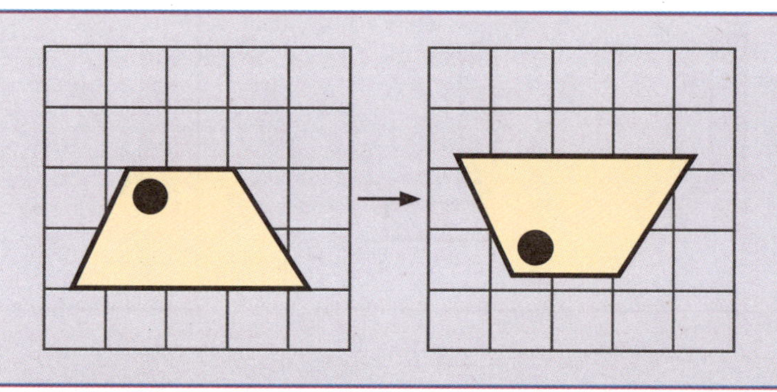

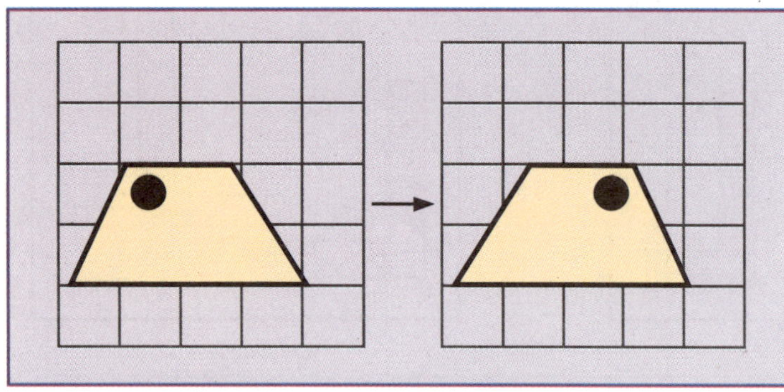

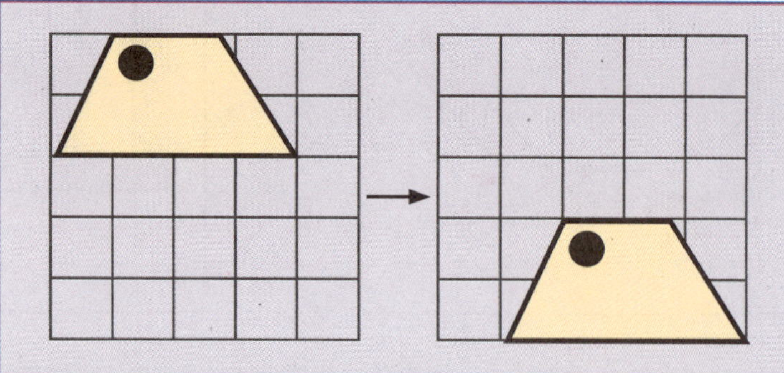

CHALLENGE

You looked at the greengrocer's window with the sign "POTATOES". When you went in and looked from the other side, how would you see "POTATOES" written? Write the word here.

Transforming Shapes

Put a tick (✓) on the figures that show turn.

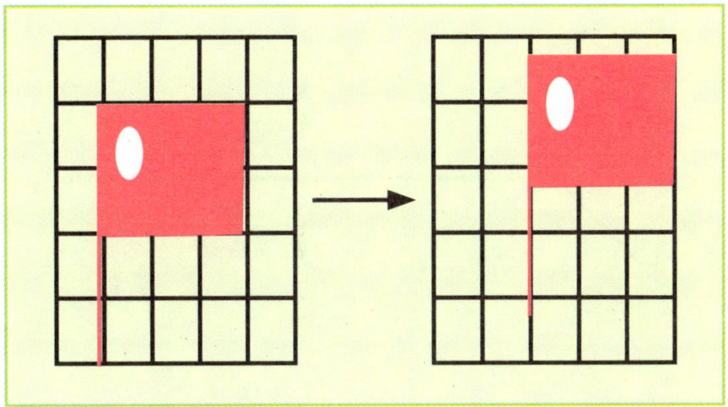

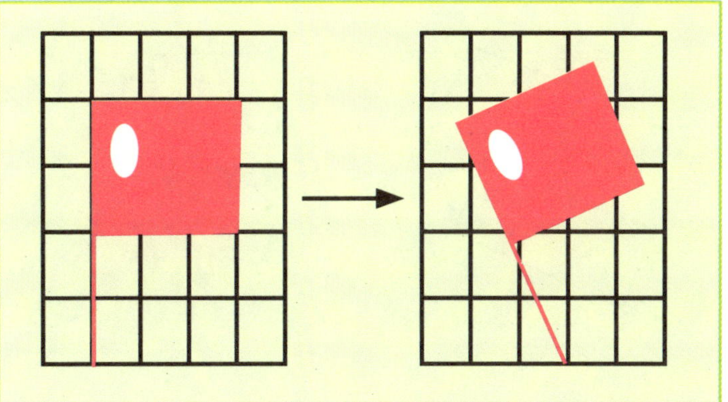

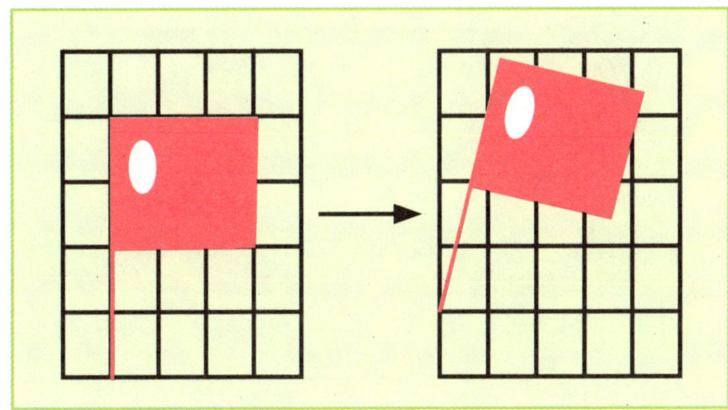

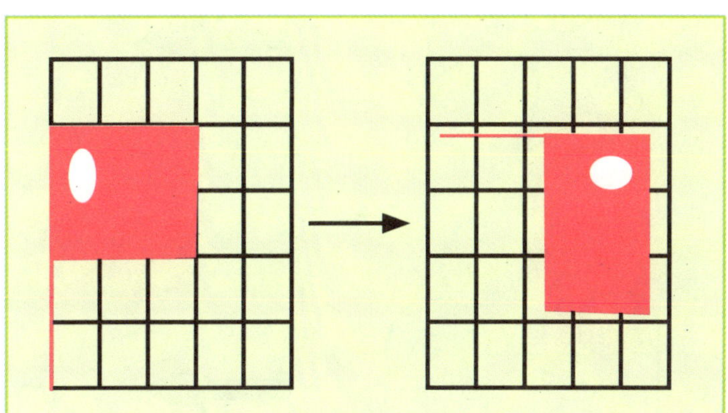

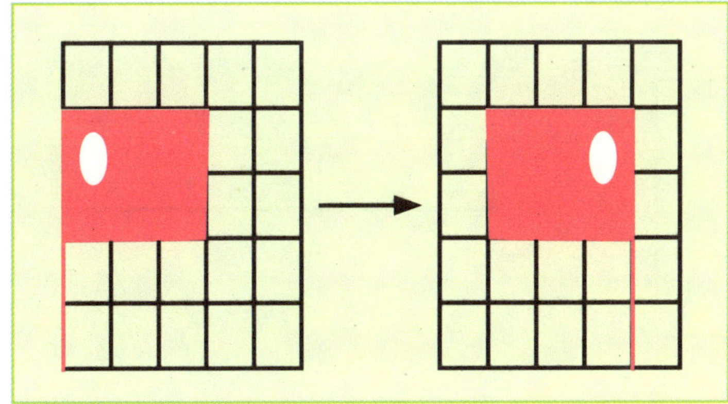

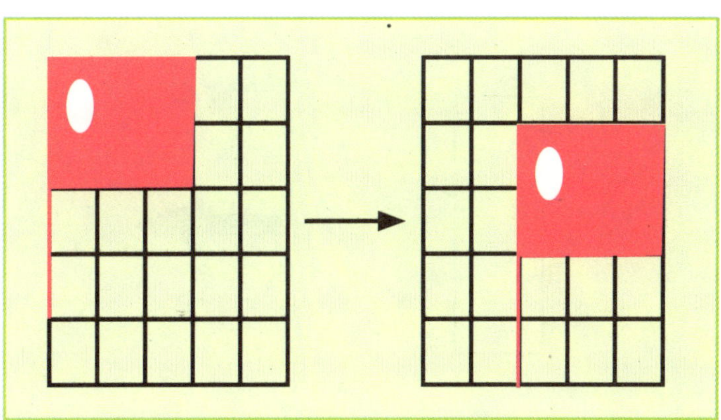

CHALLENGE

How many times will you turn this figure so that it comes back to the same position as it is in the first picture?

Transforming Shapes

For each shape, write flip, slide or turn to describe how the shape is transformed.

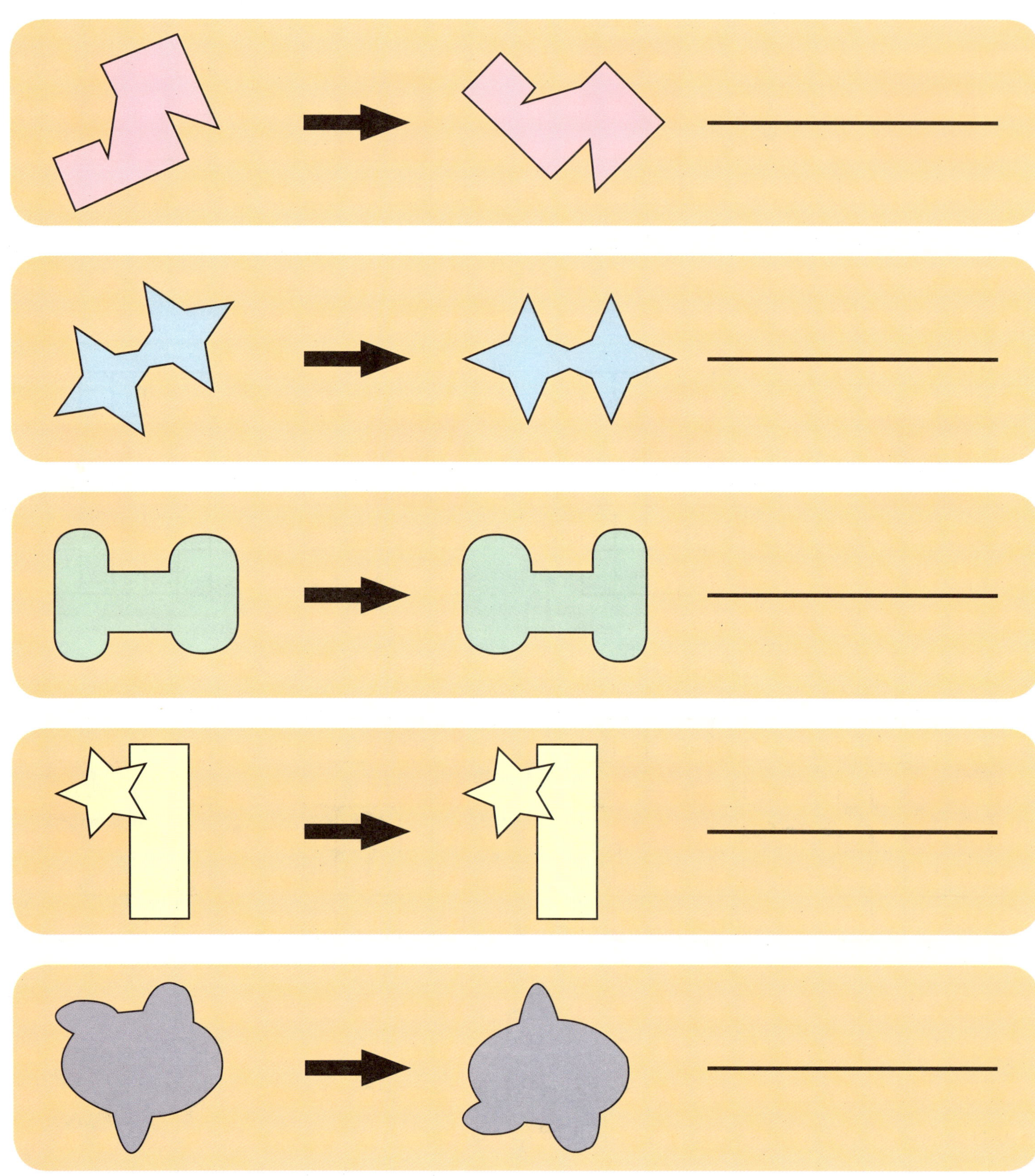

Transforming Shapes

Transform these shapes according to the instructions.

Transforming Shapes

Draw the next figure in each pattern. Write flip, slide and turn to tell what you did.

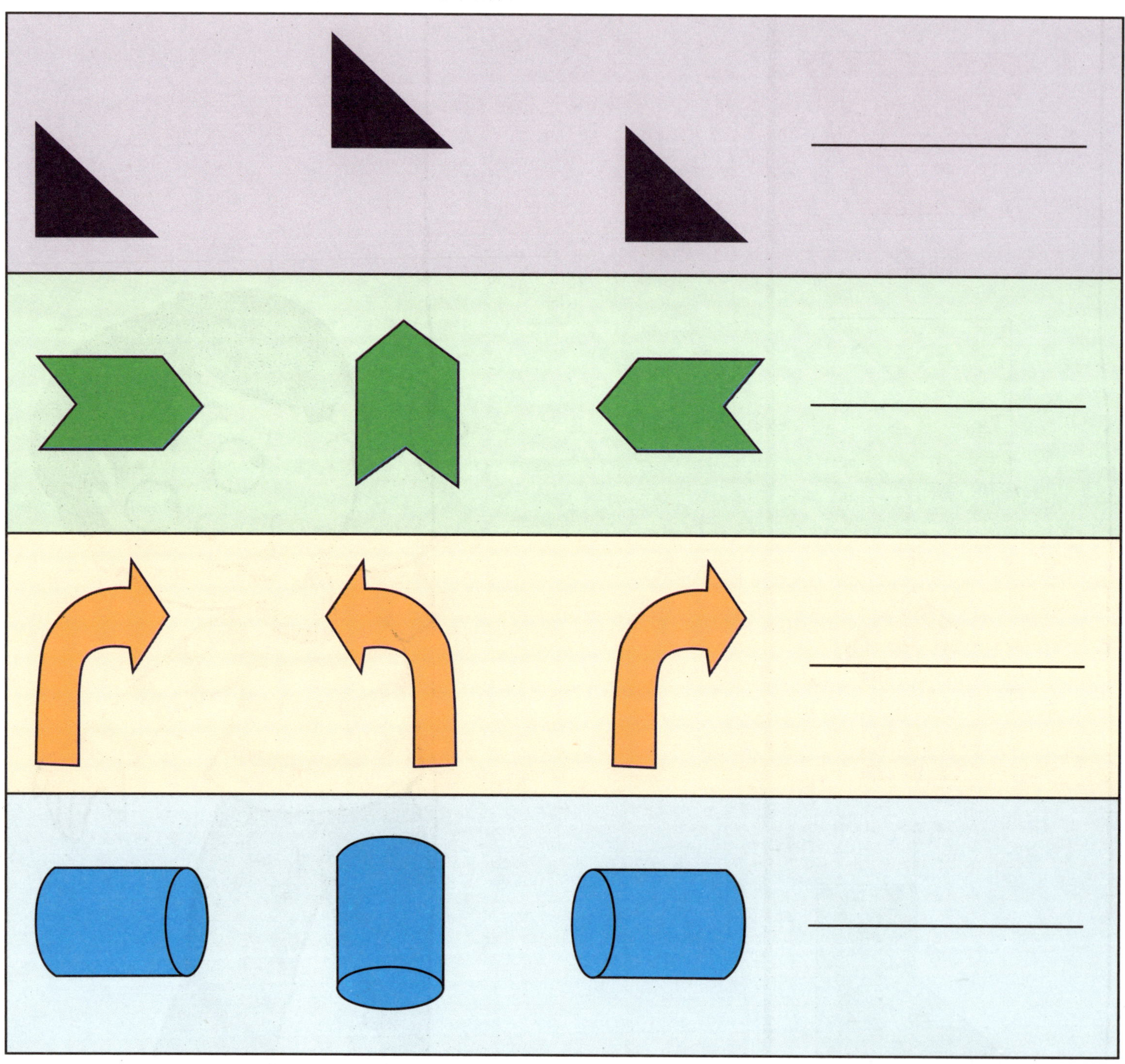

CHALLENGE

Jack created a symmetrical pattern by shading in four squares on a 3 by 3 square grid. Make a pattern of your own by using the same grid.

Page 2

1. 20 2. 3 3. $\overline{BC}$

Page 3

1. Two 2. Ray
3. AB 4. Line segment
5. Points

Page 5

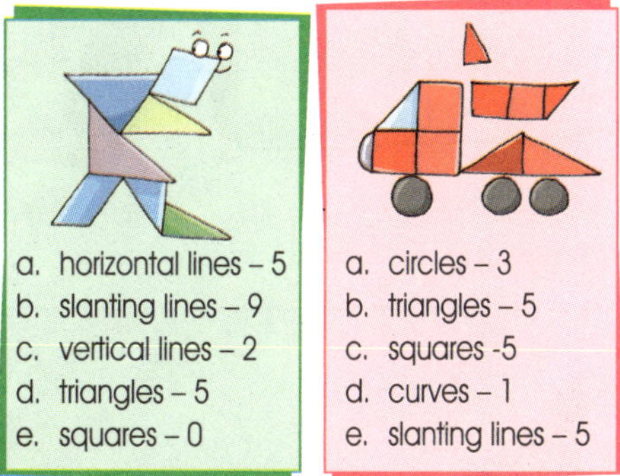

Page 6

a. Parallel
b. Parallel
c. Perpendicular
d. Parallel

Page 7

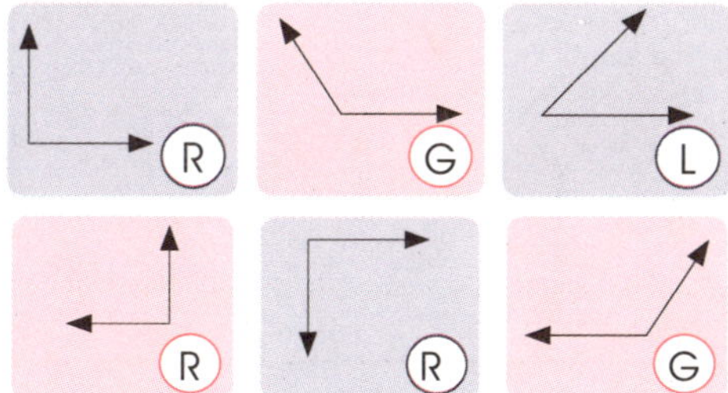

Page 8

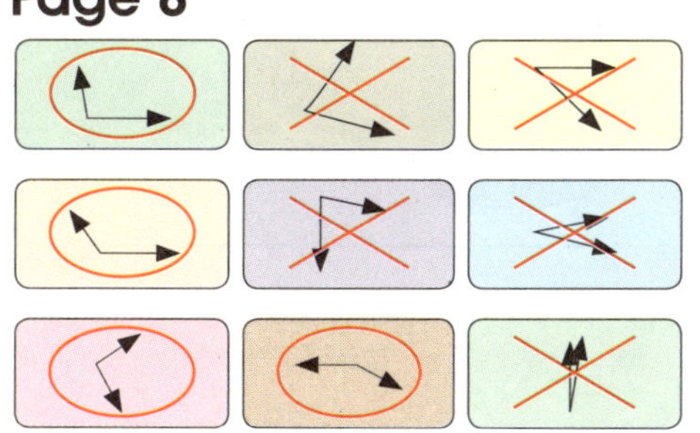

Page 9

Page 10

Page 11

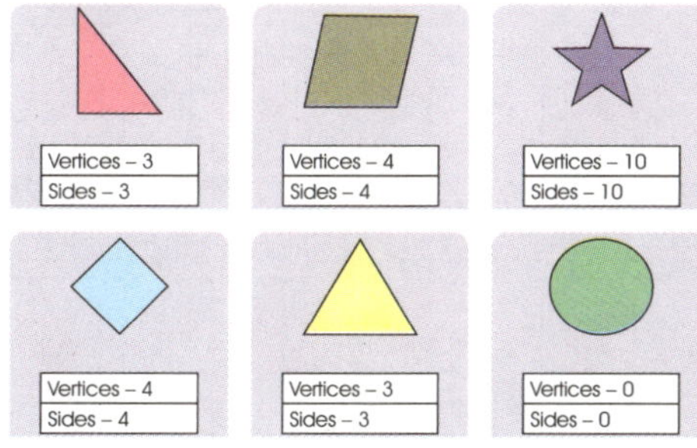

Page 13

1. A polygon with all right angles and all sides equal- television screen (is a square)
2. A polygon with only one pair of parallel sides- lamp top (is a trapezium)
3. A polygon with six sides- clock (is a hexagon)
4. A polygon with opposite sides equal - body of the truck (is a rectangle)

Page 14

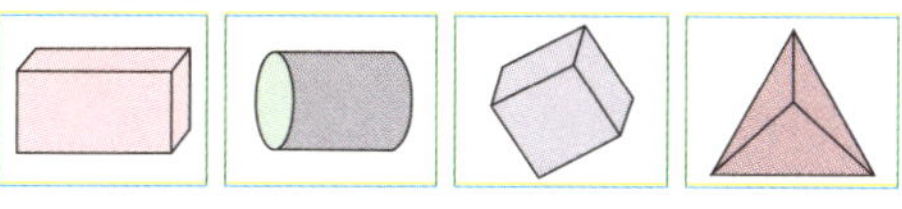

Page 16

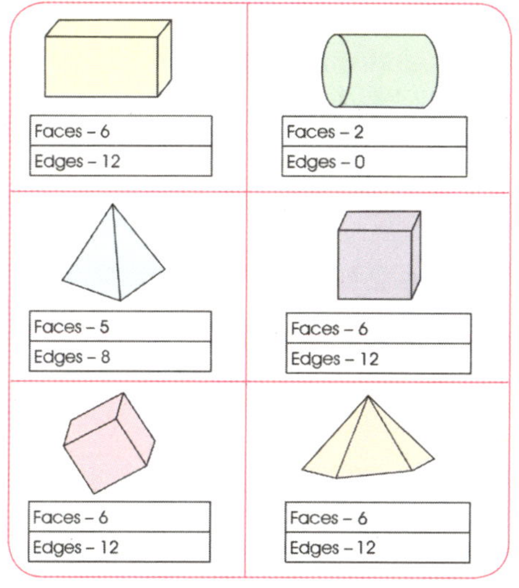

Page 18

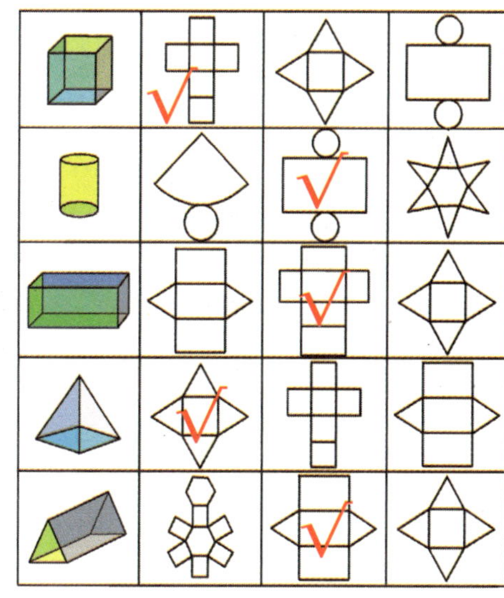

Answer Key

Page 19

Page 20

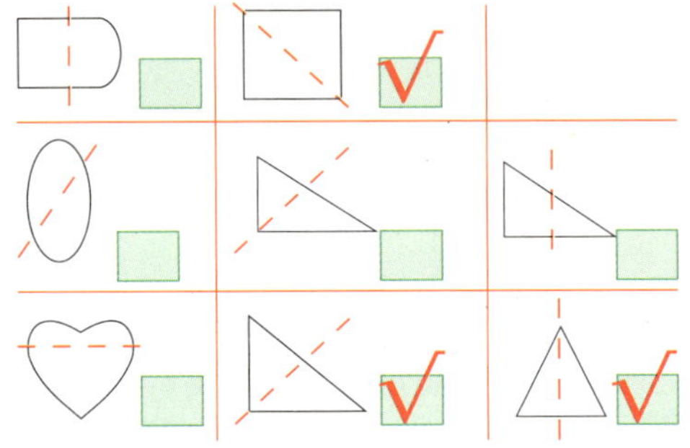

Page 21

Children to do on their own. Answers may vary.

Page 22

Children to do on their own. Answers may vary.

Page 23

Children to do on their own. Answers may vary

Page 24

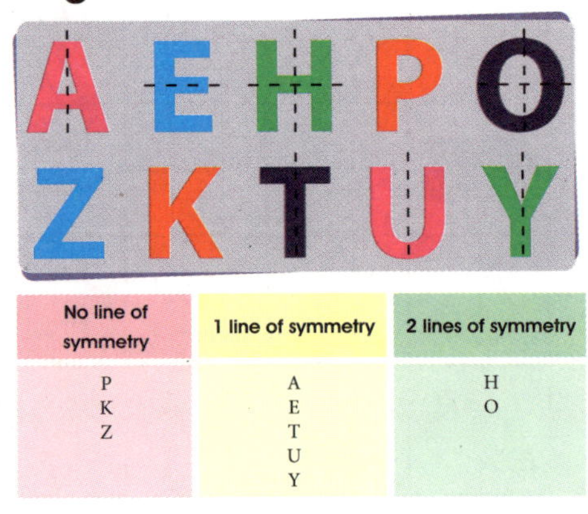

No line of symmetry	1 line of symmetry	2 lines of symmetry
P K Z	A E T U Y	H O

Page 25

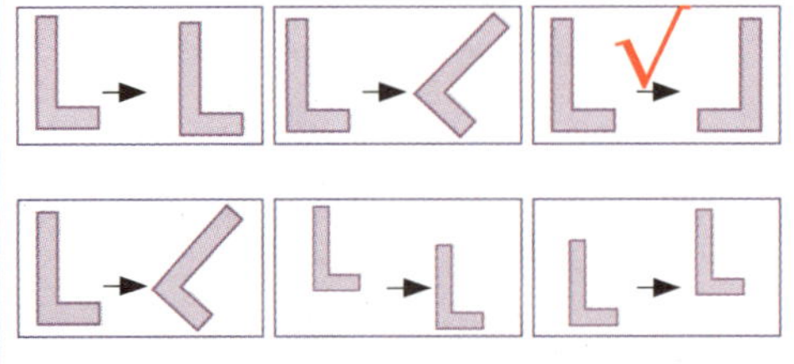

Page 26

Page 27

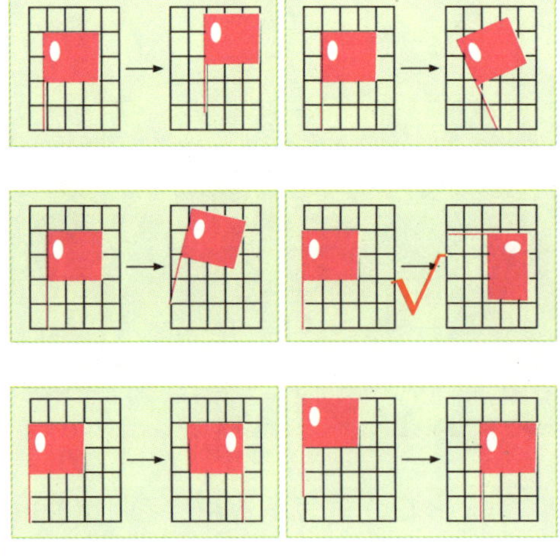

Page 28

1. Turn
2. Turn
3. Flip
4. Slide
5. Turn

Page 29

Page 30